"A SUBLIME SHOPPING SPREE"

"A sublime shopping spree. Judith McQuown shares privileged information with great style and verve. Investing in this book and its bargain buys can save you the price of a ticket!"
—Ann McGovern, publisher, *The Privileged Traveler*

"Judith McQuown's meticulously researched, clearly written book will be invaluable for the dedicated shopper."
—Robert S. Kane, author of *Britain At Its Best*

"As long as you have room in your suitcase…*Keep One Suitcase Empty* is worth taking on your next trip to Great Britain and Ireland. Judith McQuown obviously has done much of her research in person and is able to recommend transportation, warn against stores that don't take credit cards….A bonus in the guide is McQuown's own good taste—evident in her description of every store."
—Geoffrey N. Smith, editor, *Financial World*

Keep One
Suitcase
Empty

Also by Judith H. McQuown

Inc. Yourself: How to Profit by Setting Up Your Own Corporation

Tax Shelters That Work for Everyone

The Fashion Survival Manual

Playing the Takeover Market

How to Profit After You Inc. Yourself

Keep One Suitcase Empty:

The Bargain Shopper's Guide to the Best Factory Outlets in England, Ireland, Scotland, and Wales

Judith H. McQuown

ARBOR HOUSE, *New York*

Manufactured in the United States of America

10 9 8 7 6 5 4 3 2 1

Library of Congress Cataloging-in-Publication Data

McQuown, Judith H.
  Keep one suitcase empty.

  Includes index.
  1. Shopping—Great Britain—Directories.   2. Shopping
—Ireland (Eire)—Directories.   I. Title.
TX335.M393   1987   381'.45'0002541   86-28737
ISBN: 0-87795-882-3

For my mother, who taught me how to shop,
and
For my husband, who (enthusiastically) puts up with it

Shopping is an art form.
—McQuown

Contents

Acknowledgments

For their advice, help, and enthusiasm, I am grateful to the following people:

Bedford Pace and Robin Prestage of the British Tourist Authority in New York and Peter Ffrench-Hodges of the British Tourist Authority in London; John Lampl and Irene Mann of British Airways; Paul Weiss and Patricia Titley of British Rail; Claire Fitton of Staffordshire Roundabouts in Stoke-on-Trent; Gayle Drewitt of the City of Nottingham; Gina Poulter of Bradford Economic Development Unit; John Stuart of the Scottish Tourist Board; Patricia Hartley of Highland Craftpoint; Orla MacCurtain of the Irish Tourist Board in New York and Paddy Derivan of the Irish Tourist Board in Dublin; Patrick Hanrahan of Aer Lingus; and Olga Davies of the Wales Tourist Board.

For their unflagging support when *Keep One Suitcase Empty* expanded into two volumes, I am deeply grateful to Robin Rue, my agent, and to Liza Dawson, my editor.

As always, I am grateful to my husband, Harrison Roth, and to my stepdaughter, Jessica Roth, for their love and patience with my frantic travel and writing schedules.

Author's Note
𝕰𝖔𝖃𝖔𝖃𝖔𝖃𝖔𝕰

When I started researching this book, it was going to cover only factory outlets and mill shops. But as I continued my research, I found that construct was too limiting. I found that I had to include designers and artisans of all kinds who would sell directly to the public at prices far below retail. Obviously, the line blurs when the "factory" is a one- or two-person operation in the back of the store. The same thinking led me to include local crafts centers, which, because of their nonprofit status, also sold beautiful and unusual merchandise at less than retail prices.

Some favorite designers and shops may be conspicuous by their absence. In most cases, I haven't overlooked them—I've discarded them. For example, if you visit Portree on the Isle of Skye in Scotland, you'll find that I have written about the James Pringle Woollen Mills, but not about Over the Rainbow, a local knitwear designer. I debated writing about Over the Rainbow, whose styles I like very much, but finally decided that their prices of £175 for most silk/angora or silk sweaters were too expensive, compared to Hillary Rohde's and Devra King's prices for pure, heavy cashmere sweaters or Francine Dunkley's prices for silk and mohair blends.

Similarly, while many shoppers swear by the bargains they find at the Westaway & Westaway four-store complex in London's Great Russell Street, I have found better-priced sources for all the knitwear carried by Westaway & Westaway.

A brief word about prices in this book. The enormous swings in rates of exchange in the past few years that saw the British pound drop to $1.05 (in 1985) and bounce back to $1.58 (in 1986) were a clear signal that it would be foolhardy to use contemporary dollar equivalents in discussing prices in Great Britain and Ireland. Instead, it makes much more sense to leave prices in their own currency and only occasionally convert them to dollars to compare them to U.S. prices for identical items. I've used 1986 prices in the book.

Index

BY LOCATION

The Rest of Scotland

BY ITEM

Accessories

England

London

Nottingham

Cashmeres

England
London
N. Peal 38

Nottingham
CoxMoore of England 72

Bradford
British Mohair Spinners 78, 91, 94

Stanmoor Textiles Ltd. 82

Suit Length Centre 83

Texere Yarns 84

Golden Shuttle (Parkland) 89

Acres Knitwear 90

The Llama Shop 95

Johnson & Booth 96

Scotland
Edinburgh
James Pringle Woollen Mill Ltd. 121

Hillary Rohde 123

The Borders
Peter Anderson of Scotland 131

Charles N. Whillans 135, 138

Valerie Louthan Limited 135

Tom Scott Knitwear Manufacturer 136

The Weensland Spinning Company 137

White of Hawick 139

Todd & Duncan Mill Shop 144

Robert Noble & Co. Ltd. 145

Glasgow
Lomondside Knitwear Ltd. 149

The Highlands and Islands
Flora MacDonald 152

James Pringle Woollen Mill Ltd. 155

The Rest of Scotland
Inverallan Hand Knitters Limited 178

The Mill Shop 181

Devra King 185

Ireland
The Rest of Ireland
Shannon Airport Duty-free Store 232

China/Pottery/Ceramics

Clothing—Children

England

Nottingham
William Hollins "Viyella"
  70, 74

Bradford
Golden Shuttle
  (Parkland) 89

The Rest of England
J. Sheldon & Co. Ltd 104

Scotland

Edinburgh
Ewe Nique Knitwear 118
James Pringle Woollen
  Mill Ltd. 121

The Borders
Gala Sheepskin Crafts
  132
Tom Scott Knitwear
  Manufacturer 136

Glasgow
Antartex Ltd. 146, 148

*The Highlands and
  Islands*
James Pringle Woollen
  Mill Ltd. 156, 161

Isle of Sanday Knitters
  (Orkney) Ltd. 168
Reawick (Shetland)
  Lamb Marketing
  Company Ltd 173

The Rest of Scotland
Inverallan Hand Knitters
  Limited 178
The Mill Shop 181

Wales

Canolfan Cynllun Crefft
  Cymru 199
Rhoscolyn Knitwear
  205

Ireland

Dublin
Cleo Ltd. 219
Dublin Woollen Mills
  221

The Rest of Ireland
Knitwear by Phyllis
  O'Meara Ltd. 235
Campbell's of Glenties
  237
Cottage Handcrafts 240

Clothing—Men

see also Knitwear—Men

England
London
Marks & Spencer 34

Nottingham
William Hollins "Viyella"
  70, 74

Clothing—Women

see also Accessories; Knitwear—Women; Lingerie

Cosmetics/Toiletries

Crafts

Crystal and Glass

Fabrics

Foods

England

London
Marks & Spencer 34

Scotland

Edinburgh
James Pringle Woollen
Mill Ltd. 121

The Highlands and Islands
James Pringle Woollen
Mill Ltd. 155, 161

Ireland

The Rest of Ireland
Honeysuckle Products
227

Giftware

England

Stoke-on-Trent/ Staffordshire
Bull in a China Shop 49
Coalport Gift Shop 50
Mason's Ironstone 51
Staffordshire Enamels
Ltd. 58
Wedgwood Visitor
Centre 60

Nottingham
Goosefayre 64

Bradford
British Mohair Spinners
78, 91, 94
The British Wool Shop
79
Suit Length Centre 83

The Rest of England
Angora Silver Plate Co.
Ltd. 99
Stuart & Sons Ltd. 102

Scotland

Edinburgh
Adrian Hope and Linda
Lewin 119
James Pringle Woollen
Mill Ltd. 121
Scottish Craft Centre
125

The Borders
Gala Sheepskin Crafts 132
Lindean Mill Glass 134
Douglas Hunter Ceramic
Tile 140

Jewelry

England

Scotland

The Highlands and Islands

Wales

Ireland

Knitwear—Men

see also Clothing—Men

England

Knitwear—Women

see also Clothing—Women

England

Scotland

Linens

England

Stoke-on-Trent/ Staffordshire
Bull in a China Shop 49

Nottingham
Goosefayre 64
William Hollins "Viyella"
70, 74

Ireland

The Rest of Ireland
Vonnie Reynolds 231
Shannon Airport
Duty-free Store 232

Lingerie

England
Marks & Spencer 34

Nottingham
Goosefayre 64
David Nieper Ltd. 67

Bradford
Damart Thermolactyl 86

Liquor

Ireland

The Rest of Ireland
Shannon Airport
Duty-free Store 232

Picture Frames and Boxes

England

Stoke-on-Trent
Staffordshire Enamels
Ltd. 58

Birmingham
Angora Silver Plate Co.
Ltd. 99

Wales
Paul Môrafon Pewter
207

Pipes and Tobacco

Ireland

Dublin
Kapp & Peterson Ltd.
  223

Quilts/Textile Art

England

London
South Bank Crafts
  Centre 39

H. Griffiths & Son
  206
Tregwynt Textiles
  208

Wales

Brambles 198
Roger and Janet Quilter
  201

Ireland

The Rest of Ireland
Ballycar Design 231
Avoca Handweavers 245

Shoes-Custom Made

England

London
T. Savva 39

Silver

see also Jewelry

England

London
South Bank Crafts
  Centre 39

The Rest of England
Angora Silver Plate Co.
  Ltd. 99

Scotland

Edinburgh
Adrian Hope and Linda
  Lewin 119

*The Highlands and
  Islands*
Ortak Jewellery 170

Sundials

Wales
Jakim Artifacts 196

Toys and Dolls

England

London
David Evans & Co. 46

Bradford
The British Wool Shop
79

Scotland

Edinburgh
Maggie Belle Designs
120
Scottish Craft Centre
125

The Borders
Gala Sheepskin Crafts
132
Norman Cherry 141

The Highlands and Islands
Aultbea Toys 150

The Rest of Scotland
Highland Character
Dolls 186

Wales

Gwent
Pandy Craft Shop/Pandy
Play Pals 203

Ireland

Dublin
Cleo Ltd. 219
Wooden Wonders 225

The Rest of Ireland
Jean's Craft Shop Ltd.
237
Avoca Handweavers 245

Yarn

England

Bradford
British Mohair Spinners
78, 91, 94

The British Wool Shop
79

Falcon Woolshop 80

Texere Yarns 84

The Rest of England
Le Tricoteur & Co. Ltd.
101

Scotland

Edinburgh
James Pringle Woollen
Mill Ltd. 121

The Borders
Bernat Klein Limited
Studio Shop 133

The Weensland Spinning
Company 137

Francine Dunkley 142

Todd & Duncan Mill
Shop 144

The Highlands and Islands
James Pringle Woollen
Mill Ltd. 155, 161

Clansman Mill Shop 158

Skye Venture Cottage
Industry 164

The Rest of Scotland
The Mill Shop 181

Ireland

Dublin
Cleo Ltd. 219

Dublin Woollen Mills
221

The Rest of Ireland
Dripsey Woollen Mills,
Ltd. 234

Cleo Ltd. 239

Curlew Designs 243

Avoca Handweavers 245

Heather Wools Ltd. 247

List of Maps

Part One

Getting Ready

Chapter 1 Introduction

There isn't a shopper alive who wouldn't love to buy Spode china for $65 a place setting instead of $262, or a Baccarat goblet for $20 instead of $80, or a Ballantyne hand-knitted cashmere sweater for $98 instead of $450! These are but three of the many superb bargains that will be covered in *Keep One Suitcase Empty*.

For most tourists, hunting down bargains and bringing back the loot is what European travel is all about. However, most tourists settle for second-best bargains because they don't know where the factory outlets are.

This book will change all that. Just as savvy New Yorkers know where to buy wholesale, *Keep One Suitcase Empty* will give you detailed knowledge of where the British and Irish factory outlets, mill shops, and crafts centers, are, how to get to them, what to buy, and what to avoid.

Ignore the $400 duty-free exemption. When duty on sterling silver is only 7 percent, it makes sense to buy all your silver abroad, rather than at home. In fact, duty on most imports is only 7–10 percent—and that's based on the factory-outlet price you've paid in Europe!

Luxuries needn't be expensive—a point that most people don't realize. The brilliance of Baccarat, the satiny luster of Lalique, the slither of silk, the suppleness of suede—they're delightfully and amazingly affordable . . . if you know where to shop, and *Keep One*

Suitcase Empty will show you scores of factory outlets, mill shops, and craft workshops where you can buy all those delicious luxuries at prices less than one-sixth to one-third of U.S. retail prices. With such bargains you can certainly indulge all your sybaritic cravings.

Are you an armchair traveler? Don't despair! Many of the shops and factory outlets *do* sell mail order at the same superb savings as if you'd shopped there in person. In fact, one supershop, Reject China, whose name is now a misnomer for its first-quality merchandise, even tours a half-dozen U.S. cities every fall to take Christmas orders. To find out whether the shop of your choice sells through mail order, just look at the top of its listing. If it doesn't sell mail order, but you know exactly what you want, write anyway (remember to include the country's name in the address). The store may have changed its policy recently, or it may sell to you directly as a one-time favor that will generate the kind of PR that no advertisement could ever buy.

Millions of Americans will be visiting and shopping in Great Britain and Ireland this year. This book will give you a competitive edge. Happy hunting!

Chapter 2 *Before You Go*

Preparation can make the difference between an easy, happy, and successful trip and a miserable one, where everything went "just a little bit wrong." That's why it's important to spend as much time preparing for your trip as on the trip itself. From working out alternative itineraries to packing properly and contingency planning, everything you do before you leave will affect your trip. Don't wait until the last minute and then find that your passport has expired and renewing it will take five or six hours of your time and weeks of bureaucratic paper pushing. Make a checklist and mark off every item as you do it.

There are two major ways to approach planning your trip to the British Isles. One, beloved by super-shoppers and people who are furnishing a home, is to start with what they want to buy and then to travel where the buys are. The second is to choose the destination first, then ask, "What can I buy there?"

Using the first strategy can save thousands of dollars—enough for several pleasure trips or for more shopping—but it requires the dedication of a general, or at least a quartermaster, for several hours a week starting a few months before your trip. You'll become familiar enough with the ins and outs of customs regulations to send dozens of packages home duty-free while keeping your $400 allowance intact. You'll learn how to buy thousands of dollars' worth of clothing, china, silver, crystal, glassware, jewelry—all duty-free.

The second method will probably save you hundreds of dollars, rather than thousands, because your travel is more important than your shopping. But you won't have to plan as diligently, either. Just go over the basics, then concentrate on the chapters for the places to which you're traveling.

Let's start with the ground rules for bringing back your bounty.

GETTING ACCUSTOMED TO CUSTOMS

As long as you've been out of the country at least 48 hours and have not used the customs exemption in the last 30 days, the first $400 of your purchases are duty-free. The next $1,000 are taxed at a flat 10 percent. Purchases over $1,400 are taxed at specific rates; for example, sterling silver carries a duty of 7 percent.

I feel that you bargain hunters should ignore the issue of customs duty for these reasons:

- Most duty rates are less than 10 percent.
- If you bought the same merchandise in the United States, you'd still be paying that duty; it would be included in the retail price.
- The $400 and $1,000 limitations are based on *your cost;* therefore, because your purchase prices are so low, you'll be able to buy much more before you exceed those limits.
- If you have gone over the $1,400 limit, you can group your purchases so that the items that would be subject to the highest duty fall into the under $1,400 category and the items that are subject to the lowest duty fall into the over $1,400 category. Customs officials will help you calculate the minimum duty you have to pay.

FREEBIES

If you've made a large purchase that's easily divisible—like a china or silver service—you can have it sent home piecemeal, duty-free, in batches that cost less than $50, as unsolicited gifts. Many manufacturers and merchants of items usually purchased in multiples are particularly adept at manipulating this rule to your benefit. For example, you can buy a service for twelve in Spode's Consul, a pattern that costs around $48 per place setting when purchased in the factory-outlet shops in Stoke-on-Trent, England's china center (see Chapter 5 for details), and $220 in New York. You give the store the names of your spouse, your two children living with you, and three cooperative neighbors. The store wraps a package of three place settings and sends them to your home, listing the three members of your family as recipients, and stamping "Gift: Value Under $50" next to each name, and similarly wraps and marks the package of three place settings to be sent to your neighbors.

Three or four days later, to ensure that the packages won't arrive on the same day—and thus be subject to customs duty—the store sends out the remaining six place settings: three to your family and three to your neighbors. The result: you receive your china service for twelve duty-free at a savings of approximately $2,064 over U.S. retail prices.

If you chose a more expensive pattern, the store would break up a five-piece place setting so that the value of each batch of china would remain under $50 and simply would send more packages. Shipping costs would increase slightly, but you'd still pay no duty.

Reentry Problems:

Bringing Home the
Triple-wood-smoked
Bacon

Luxury shopping includes gourmet foods—often bargains in their native countries. Customs and agricultural regulations can be very tricky in this area, so if there's a specific delicacy you'd like to bring back that is not mentioned here or in the U.S. Department of Agriculture's brochure *Traveler's Tips on Bringing Food, Plant, and Animal Products into the United States,* write to the Animal and Plant Health and Inspection Service of the nearest branch of the Department of Agriculture, and carry with you the letter granting permission to show the agricultural inspector when you return through customs with your delicious prize.

In general, most delicacies are admitted without any problem, so stock up on sides of Irish and Scotch smoked salmon (they *do* taste different) and on slabs of smoky Irish bacon. Make sure that the country of origin is labeled clearly and that the wrapping has not been broken.

Canned and baked goods and candies are fine, as are most spices. Take advantage of the recently relaxed customs prohibition against bringing home liqueur-filled chocolates, which are available freely all over Europe. Now you can bring in an undefined, "sensible" quantity—limited only by what you can carry home in last-minute shopping. I've had no trouble bringing home a dozen 3½-ounce bars and two or three boxed assortments.

Sausages may pose a problem, and you should get a ruling in writing before trying to smuggle in one of Bologna's famed mortadellas, as Sophia Loren was caught doing in the comedy film *Mortadella.*

To enter the United States, most products that contain beef, pork, or lard must be canned and shelf-stable, and must have a certificate from their government stating that they have passed certain tests. Cheeses must be aged and cured, not fresh.

The rules and regulations of the U.S. Department of Agriculture change periodically, so if you're thinking of bringing back unusual gourmet goodies, check with the department before your trip.

Drinkables

It's probably a good idea to take advantage of your ability to bring in 1 liter (33.8 ounces) of liquor duty-free. Duty on additional liquor runs $12.50 to $15 per gallon, depending on the type and price, but duty on wine is only *60 to 80 cents per gallon.*

The wine-loving bargain hunter in me is torn between recommending that you buy as much wine as you can lug around comfortably and cautioning you that lugging wine around is very exhausting and that wine takes up room in your luggage that you might want and need for other bargains you've purchased. It can also make you exceed your baggage allowance so that you have to pay the extra freight.

If you think you might be buying a dozen cases of wine, you may want to sail back rather than fly back. That way you won't have to worry about excess baggage.

Making Scents

Don't think you can automatically bring home gallons of your favorite fragrance. Some perfume companies are more restrictive than others in letting you bring their products from abroad. They limit you to one bottle each of perfume, cologne, and toilet water. The list may change, so it's a good idea to check with U.S. Customs Trademark Information before you leave. At last count, here are some well-known fragrances that are restricted to the one-bottle rule and some that are not:

No restriction	*One bottle each of perfume, cologne, etc.*
Chantilly	Bellodgia
Dior	Chamade
Dioressence	Chanel No. 2
Diorissimo	Chanel No. 5
Eau de Rochas	Chanel No. 19
Femme	Chanel No. 22
Hermès	Chanel No. 55
Madame Rochas	Chant D'Arômes
Miss Dior	Guerlain
Monsieur Rochas	Habit Rouge de Guerlain
Nina Ricci	Joy
Opium	L'Heure Bleue
Rive Gauche	Mitsouko
YSL	Shalimar

Your Own Things

Are you traveling with your mink? Rolex? Minolta? Register them with your local customs office before you leave the United States or carry proof of prior ownership (bill of sale, insurance policy, appraisal statement) with you—or face paying duty on them when you return.

It's easy to register items with serial numbers, like watches or cameras, but you must bring them with you and register them in person. The customs office will issue you a Certificate of Registration for Personal Effects Taken Abroad that is valid for all your future trips.

Without this certificate, you still may be able to avoid paying duty by showing, through a check of serial or model numbers, that your possession is several years old, but don't bet on it. It's just as likely for your customs inspector to decide that you've bought a secondhand watch or camera on your trip and to tax you accordingly.

Keep a copy of the certificate at home for safekeeping. You'll need to carry the original with you on every trip that you take the items you have registered. Before departure, you must present the certificate and the articles covered to a customs officer for comparison and signing of the form. You must also present them to a customs officer upon your return.

NATIONAL TOURIST OFFICES

Having briefed you on customs, it's time to turn to the British and Irish national tourist offices in the United States, excellent sources of information. Contact them early and often as you plan your trip, and try to get all the information you need before June, the beginning of the peak tourist season. The more specific your questions, the better advice you'll receive.

Great Britain (includes
Scotland and Wales)
    British Tourist Authority:
    40 West 57th Street
    New York, NY 10019
    (212) 581–4700

    612 South Flower Street
    Los Angeles, CA 90017
    (213) 623–8196

    John Hancock Center
    875 North Michigan Avenue, Suite 3320
    Chicago, IL 60611
    (312) 787–0490

Plaza of the Americas
North Tower, Suite 750
Lock Box 346
Dallas, TX 75201
(214) 748–2279

Ireland

Irish Tourist Board:
757 Third Avenue
New York, NY 10017
(212) 418–0800

Century Park East
Suite 314
Los Angeles, CA 90067
(213) 557–0722

681 Market Street
San Francisco, CA 94105
(415) 781–5688

230 North Michigan Avenue
Chicago, IL 60601
(312) 726–9356

European Sizes

This part is so crucial to your trip that you should copy these tables and keep them in your purse in case you're ever caught without the book. You'll use them often.

Sizes will vary slightly from manufacturer to manufacturer—to say nothing of from country to country. That's the reason I recommend carrying a measuring tape with you. Most have metric measurements on one side, but that's not important. What *is* important is the side with inches-and-feet measurements.

Men

Suits and Overcoats

American/Canadian/ British/Irish	36	38	40	42	44	46	48
}	36	38	40	42	44	46	48

Shirts

American/Canadian/ British/Irish }	14	14½	15	15½	16	16½	17	17½

Shoes

American/Canadian	6½	7½	8½	9½	10½	11½
British/Irish	6	7	8	9	10	11

Socks

American/Canadian/ British/Irish }	9½	10	10½	11	11½	12	12½

Hats and Caps

	6⅞	7	7⅛	7¼	7⅜	7½	7⅝	7¾
American/Canadian/ British/Irish }								

Women
Suits and Dresses

	6⅞	7	7⅛	7¼	7⅜	7½	7⅝	7¾
American	6	8	10	12	14	16	18	20
Canadian	8	10	12	14	16	18	20	22
British/Irish	30	32	34	36	38	40	42	44

Sweaters

American/Canadian	30	32	34	36	38	40	42	44
British/Irish	76	81	86	91	97	102	107	112

Shoes

American	4½	5	5½	6	6½	7	7½	8	8½	9
Canadian	5	5½	6	6½	7	7½	8	8½	9	9½
British/Irish	3	3½	4	4½	5	5½	6	6½	7	7½

Stockings and Socks

American/Canadian } British/Irish	8	8½	9	9½	10	10½	11

Hats

American/Canadian } British/Irish	21½	22	22⅜	22¾	23⅛	23½	24

Gloves   Sizes are the same

More Useful Metric Information

These equivalent measurements will come in handy when you're buying food and beverages, gasoline, and fabric, and when you're calculating distances:

U.S. → Metric
1 ounce = 28.35 grams
¼ pound = 113.4 grams
½ pound = 226.8 grams
1 pound = 453.6 grams = .45 kilogram

Metric → U.S.
1 gram = 0.035 ounce
100 grams = 3.5 ounces
250 grams = 8.75 ounces
500 grams = 17.5 ounces (1.1 pounds)
1 kilogram (1,000 grams) = 2.2 pounds

1 quart = .95 liter
1 gallon = 3.80 liters

1 liter = 33.8 fluid ounces (1.06 quarts)
10 liters = 2.64 gallons
40 liters = 10.56 gallons

1 inch = 2.54 centimeters
1 foot = 0.30 meter
1 yard = 0.91 meter

1 centimeter = 0.39 inch
1 meter = 39.4 inches = 1.09 yards

1 mile = 1.61 kilometers
10 miles = 16 kilometers
50 miles = 81 kilometers
100 miles = 161 kilometers

1 kilometer (1,000 meters) = 0.62 mile
10 kilometers = 6.2 miles
50 kilometers = 31 miles
100 kilometers = 62 miles

Comparison Shop Before You Leave

To make the most of your shopping time and money on your trip, do some comparison shopping at home first. If you have already chosen your china, silver, and crystal patterns but have not yet purchased all your pieces, visit a department store that carries your patterns and jot down the pieces you want, their serial numbers, and their prices. They'll tell you whether the prices you see abroad are a bargain. Try to get the leaflets that illustrate each pattern; sometimes (fortunately, not often) patterns have one name in Europe, another in the United States.

If you are fortunate enough to live in or near a city with a large wholesale district that is accessible to savvy private shoppers, use those prices, rather than retail prices, in making your comparisons. Few situations are more irritating than discovering, after you have lugged or shipped hundreds of pounds of dinnerware, that you could have bought it locally for only slightly more than what you thought was the overseas bargain price.

A notebook organizer—Filofax or one of its clones —is an excellent tool for serious shopping. Use a separate page for everyone you'll be shopping for: measurements, favorite colors, what you plan to buy for that person. Use other pages, or even a different section, for your home. Plan your shopping room by room if you like. Tape swatches of fabrics, paint chips, color photographs of the room, clips from architectural and decorating magazines—anything that may help you decide whether that remnant of glorious English chintz will be perfect in your room or a disaster. *And make sure that you measure—and write down—the dimensions of any pieces of furniture you are planning to reupholster, windows for which you want new draperies, beds for which you crave fine European linens, blankets, quilts.* Especially the last—American beds are sized very differently from European beds.

COMPARISON SHOP FOR YOUR FARE, TOO

You can save hundreds of dollars by comparison shopping for your airfare. APEX tickets cost about half the economy fares, but are subject to restrictions and penalize travelers who change their plans.

If you are very flexible and can make last-minute plans, flying standby can be the cheapest way to go. Standby tickets to London are the most frequently offered by the greatest number of airlines, but sometimes standby tickets to other cities are also available.

You can also often find bargains through companies that specialize in offering enormous discounts in last-minute travel arrangements:

Moment's Notice
40 East 49th Street
New York, NY 10017
(212) 486–0503
(800) 253–4321

Last-Minute Travel Club
6A Glenville Avenue
Allston, MA 02134
(617) 254–5200

Adventures on Call
Box 18592
BWI Airport, MD 21240
(301) 356–4080

Discount Travel International
114 Forest Avenue
The Ives Building, Suite 205
Narberth, PA 19072
(215) 668–2182

Short Notice Trip Service
American Leisure Industries
4501 Forbes Boulevard
Lanham, MD 20706
(301) 459–8020

Stand-Buys Ltd.
311 West Superior, Suite 414
Chicago, IL 60610
(312) 943–5737

Vacations to Go
5901-D Westheimer Road
Houston, TX 77057
(713) 974–2121

Worldwide Discount Travel Club
1674 Meridian Avenue
Miami Beach, FL 33139
(305) 534–2082

These travel wholesalers charge an annual fee per family of $35 to $50, and deals are often announced only a week or two in advance; but if you can travel on the spur of the moment, you'll save hundreds of dollars on each trip.

GOOD THINGS COME IN PACKAGES

Even the most independent of travelers should investigate package tours. Many of them offer incredible value: airfare, hotel, most or all meals, entertainment—all for around the price of a round-trip ticket. Typical in 1986: the Irish Long Weekend Shopping Spree, leaving on Aer Lingus every Wednesday and returning every Sunday from fall through spring, with all meals, including a medieval banquet and a cabaret show, first-class hotels, and shopping-oriented tours, for as little as $429 from New York. If you buy a pair of Burberry raincoats, a Donegal tweed jacket, an Aran sweater, and a Waterford decanter or two, you'll actually make a profit on your trip, compared to U.S. retail prices for the same merchandise.

Similarly, in 1986 TWA had a package to London that included round-trip airfare and six nights in a hotel for only $474.

Of course, you don't have to participate in all the tour's programs. In fact, many seasoned travelers buy tour packages for the best air/hotel prices, and then go it on their own. You may wish to do likewise.

REMEMBER THE WEATHER

Before even thinking of what clothes you need for your trip, find out about the weather at your destination. It's even a good idea to call the airline or your destination country's tourist office to check the next week's long-range weather forecast just before you pack. Many Americans, used to winter temperatures of 0° to 20°F and summer temperatures of 80° to 100°F forget that Europe is more temperate—and generally cooler and milder—than most of the United States.

Great Britain is north of the United States—New York, Madrid, and Rome are virtually on the same degree of latitude. Labrador, London, and Amsterdam share almost the same degree of latitude. Their location means that the British Isles have fairly cool summers— 85°F in London is virtually a heat wave. Some years ago, I spent part of July at a writers' conference in Dublin. The weather was damp, and only 40° to 50°F. We immediately bought Aran Isle sweaters and wool socks to protect ourselves from freezing and stoked up on Irish coffee.

On the other hand, thanks to coastal currents, most European winters are milder than American winters. Snow in the cities is quite rare, and temperatures tend to range from 30° to 45°F, with little wind, but much dampness.

Think of the climate of San Francisco or Seattle, and you'll have a fair idea of what to take on your trip:

layered sweaters and a lined raincoat for winter, rather than a heavy overcoat, and one or two lightweight sweaters even in the summer.

Here's a quick rundown of average Fahrenheit temperature ranges you'll encounter.

Country	January	April	July	October
England	35°–45°	40°–60°	50°–70°	45°–60°
Ireland	35°–50°	40°–60°	50°–70°	40°–60°
Scotland	30°–40°	30°–50°	50°–70°	40°–55°
Wales	30°–40°	30°–50°	50°–70°	40°–55°

WHAT TO PACK BESIDES CLOTHING

Everyone knows about taking essentials, like passports, hotel and car-rental confirmations, driver's license, maps, spare glasses or contact lenses, prescription drugs, and copies of the prescriptions.

Here are some items you might not think of that will make the difference between an ordinary trip and a luxurious and convenient one:

- Tape measure—for measuring everything you buy and for saving try-on time by rejecting items that don't fit
- Pocket calculator—to help you see what everything *really* costs
- Swiss army knife—indispensable for eating in your room or alfresco
- Miniature salt and pepper mills—ditto
- Your favorite blend of coffee, regular tea, or herbal tea
- Packets of sugar, saccharine, or Equal
- Immersion coil for making the coffee or tea in your room. Make sure that it's designed to work on European current
- A flask of your favorite potion—I prefer Armagnac or cognac—superb sipping in the tub after a long day's shopping

- Liquid face and hand soap—less messy to travel with than a cake of soap and soap dish
- Travel alarm clock, especially if you have trains and buses to catch. I have discovered the hard way that some countries and some hotels are more casual than others about remembering the precise time of your wake-up call.
- Portable cassette player/radio and some of your favorite tapes; you'll also be able to get news and weather forecasts on the radio
- Sewing kit
- Safety pins
- Rubber bands
- Paper clips
- Tiny stapler
- Small pair of scissors
- Adhesive bandages
- Tweezers
- Folding cup
- Business cards

MONEY

Most travelers already know that traveler's checks always get a better rate of exchange than cash and that some traveler's checks are free. For example, Thomas Cook dollar-denominated traveler's checks are free if you make arrangements through their travel agency. Some banks offer free traveler's checks, too. They profit from the float—the use of your money—between the day you buy the checks and the day you cash them.

When you get your traveler's checks, copy the refund instructions and your traveler's checks' serial numbers and put them with their purchase receipt, your passport number, and date of issue, and a list of the credit cards you're carrying and their serial numbers. Tuck this envelope away in your luggage for emergency use should your wallet or purse be stolen or lost.

Many travel specialists recommend buying a "tip pack" of coins and notes of every country you'll be visiting before you leave. Because rates of exchange for these tip packs are grossly unfavorable, I think it's wiser to exchange $50 to $100. By doing so, you also save yourself having to exchange more money as soon as you arrive; you can shop around for the best rate of exchange.

Many experts also advise against exchanging dollars for foreign currency at hotels, restaurants, or shops. I agree with their point about hotels, but have found on recent trips that restaurants and retail shops often offer a slightly better rate of exchange than banks because restaurants and shops want you to *spend* your money there, rather than exchange it.

True, there are pros and cons about using credit cards themselves and praying that the rate of exchange will be favorable on the day the credit-card companies calculate what you owe them. On the other hand, virtually no matter what happens to the rate of exchange, you've usually gained around two months of float until you must pay your bill, and by shopping at the sources recommended in this book, you are paying U.S. wholesale prices, or much less.

BARGAINING STRATEGIES

Bargaining strategies are not the ones you would use in a bazaar or marketplace. Furthermore, haggling is just plain inappropriate in shops where there are neatly marked price tags.

Does this mean that it's impossible to bargain? Not at all. It means only that your bargaining strategies must be more subtle.

Buying in quantity is one good way to get bargains. If one of something costs X, surely three of them could be sold for 2.5X, six for 4.5X, and a dozen for

8.5X. After all, the shop is moving merchandise more quickly and therefore more profitably, and only one sales ticket or charge slip has to be written up—for one item or a dozen.

Offering the possibility of spending lots of money is another way. If an item is very expensive, you needn't buy a dozen in order to ask for—and receive— a price reduction. Be tentative and hesitant when you say, "I really love that. Can you do a little better on the price?" A shopkeeper who wants to make the sale may come down 10 percent; on a $500 goodie, that's $50.

If the price is firm, see whether you can gain other concessions. Will the shop send home your bulky purchase without charging you for parcel post? What about a more favorable rate of exchange than the bank is offering? Will the owner throw in a little gift? Let's say you've bought an expensive coat or suit. You'd love a coordinating silk scarf, or earrings. Get the idea?

At Last!

Before your final packing, there's just one more little thing to do. Call the airline and get as long-term a weather forecast as possible for your destination.

Now pack and check off everything on your list. Got your passport? Tickets? Measuring tape?

Bon voyage and happy shopping!

Part Two

England

Chapter 3 *England: The Basics*

When it comes to European travel, most Americans visit England first, many visit England more often than any other country, and quite a few visit England only. Is it the comfortable feeling of not having to learn a foreign language, familial roots, or a generalized Anglophilia strengthened by specific warmth toward Shakespeare, Churchill, Sherlock Holmes, and *Masterpiece Theatre*? Perhaps. But for shoppers, it's also the comfortable feeling of buying English quality and craftsmanship at its reasonably priced source.

WHAT TO BUY

Clothing—especially knitwear—natural-fiber luxury fabric and yarns, china and pottery, crystal, silver, and cutlery.

1986 CURRENCY RANGE

The rate of exchange as of mid-December 1986 for £1 varies between $1.38–$1.56. While $1.38-$1.56 may seem high compared to the 1985 low of $1.05, historically it's relatively low. From about 1970 to about 1983, the pound ranged from $2.80 to $1.75— well above where it is today.

England

England's excellent rail system makes it easy to travel around the country, amassing bargains as you go. Most cities are less than three hours' ride from London, and BritRail's InterCity 125 trains, which travel at 125 mph, will take you shopping more quickly than any car.

The VAT

A 15 percent VAT (value-added tax) is imposed on most goods, except for food, children's clothing, antiques, and many one-of-a-kind works of art, including handicrafts, which are exempt. The 15 percent VAT works out to 13.4 percent of the total purchase price.

Getting It Back

Most shops require a £50 minimum purchase, which can be made up of several items. Many shops will refund the VAT to your credit-card account if you ask the salesperson to do so. This refund procedure will save you the bother of getting a check for £6 or £7 several months hence, that your bank will charge you $10 or so for cashing—leaving you with $1 or less.

Keep invoices for your purchases in your hand baggage—you'll have to present them to a customs officer. Remember to get the VAT refund forms stamped by a customs official at Heathrow or Gatwick airports and to drop them in the special mailboxes. No customs form, no refund. And keep track of the VAT refunds due you. If they don't show up on your credit card in two or three months, write to the shop where you bought the merchandise.

You'll also have to show your purchases to customs officials at British and U.S. airports, so pack them where they are accessible—preferably in your hand baggage.

Telephone Numbers

The telephone numbers given for the shops show both the city area code and the telephone number. If you are dialing from within the same city, omit the area code, which is the number in parentheses. If you are dialing from outside the city, include it. If you are dialing from outside the country—for example, from the United States or Canada—start with the international access code (011), followed by the code for Britain (44), followed by the city code (the number shown in parentheses *minus the zero*). Thus, a call from New York to London would begin 011 44 1, while a call to Edinburgh would begin 011 44 31. But a call from London to Edinburgh would begin 031.

Chapter 4 *London*

For centuries, London has been everyone's favorite shopping city. Bond Street celebrated its tercentenary recently, and the Burlington Arcade and Regent Street are but decades younger.

Of course, everyone pops into Harrods Food Halls to pick up nibbles for the hotel room or club—to give strength between shopping forays?

The London Underground is probably the fastest way to get around town for shopping, and the fastest and best way to use the Underground is by buying the London Explorer ticket. This ticket lets you speed through the entrance and exit gates of the Underground stations and offers unlimited travel on trains and buses, including the Airbus service between Heathrow Airport and London. A one-day ticket costs £5; a three-day ticket, £15; a four-day ticket, £18; and a seven-day ticket, £24.

Whether this trip is your first or your fiftieth, I do hope that you will enjoy London more now that you have some new shopping sources.

THE BIG ONES

Boots Chemist
Branches all over Britain

*Mon.–Sat., hours vary
according to location
VISA/Barclaycard,
MasterCard/Access*

Boots rates a tiny section all its own because it has hundreds of branches all over England, Wales, and

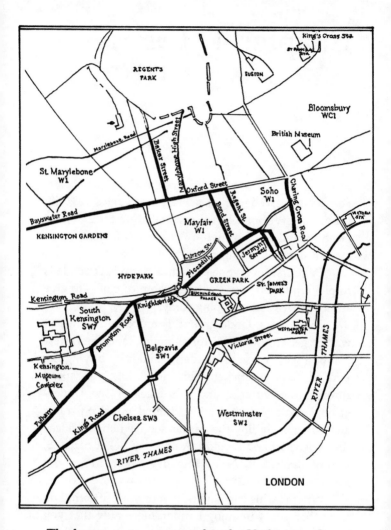

The best way to get around is the Underground. You can get a pocket map at any station. If you've got only one day for shopping, you'll do best in Mayfair, Chelsea, and South Kensington.

Scotland. Some of the chain's larger shops, such as those in Regent Street and in Piccadilly Circus in London, and in Manchester, carry computer equipment, cameras, cookware, and even baby carriages, but serious shoppers will ignore these and run right over to the makeup and skin-treatment counters.

Boots's products are superb, and they are inexpensive. Women who are used to spending $20–$25 for a bottle of foundation will be amazed at Boots's luxury line No. 7 Special Collection silky foundation for only £3.95. A translucent moisturizing powder in a handsome charcoal D-shaped compact is £4.75—comparatively expensive for Boots, but worth the price. Skin refining cream is £3.95.

The regular-line cosmetics are less expensive, with lipstick selling for £1.80, mascara for £2.25, and unusual and useful color-correcting moisturizers in green and violet, to balance skin tones, for £2.75.

Boots always has some of its cosmetics at special low prices. This time it was a 40-ml (approximately 1½-ounce) tube of No. 7 Protective Moisturiser Tint with UVA and UVB sunscreens for only £1. Several discontinued body-care products were also marked down to very low prices. The pleasantly scented Florence collection, a blend of roses, jasmine, and honeysuckle, was on sale: the 250-ml (8½-ounce) size of Moisturising Bath Foam and the 250-ml size of Rich Hand and Body Lotion were only 75p each; the 100-gram (3½-ounce) canister of talcum powder was only 55p.

Boots truly excels in bath and skin-care products; they are made of natural ingredients and are quite inexpensive. My only criticism is that they are packed in glass, so that they are too fragile and heavy to be taken home in their original packaging. They have to be decanted into plastic bottles and jars and then labeled.

Sybaritic herbal bath oils—all in 200-ml (6¾-ounce) sizes—are lovely. Choose from Seaweed and Sweet Sedge Exceptional Cream Bath (£2.25), Clover, Tansy, and Angelica Crystal Bath (£2.25), Fern and Borage Invigorating Bath Essence (£3.10), Primrose and Marigold Invigorating Bath Essence (£1.55), Bluebell and Sweet Balm Exceptional Cream Bath (£3.25), or Rose and Almond Aromatic Bath Oil for Dry Skin (£3.25). Or, at these low prices, why not take them all!

Other excellent herbal products are the Almond and Rosewater Cleanser for Normal and Dry Skin (£2.25), Peach and Almond Light Moisture Lotion (£2.55), Columbine and Almond Oil Face Mask (£1.85), Almond Oil and Lilac Extra Rich Body Lotion (£3.20), Wheatgerm and Comfrey Enriched Massage Oil (£1.47), and Buttermilk and Clover Honey Unique Skin Balm (£3.45).

Marks & Spencer

458 Oxford Street, Marble Arch
London W1
Tel. (01) 935 7954

Mon.–Sat. 9:00–6:00,
Thurs. 9:00–7:30 (branch hours may vary)
Own credit cards, traveler's checks in pounds

Marks & Spencer rates an entry in this book because it has its own subcontractors who produce to Marks & Spencer's stringent specifications. With hundreds of stores around the world, it has to subcontract, and its economies of large-scale production really benefit the consumer.

Most Brits swear by "Marks and Sparks," as they call the store affectionately, because it provides good-to excellent-quality merchandise at unbeatable prices. Whether it's men's socks or cashmere sweaters (I'm still wearing one I bought on my first trip back in 1971), the design is good, if middle of the road, and the workman-ship is excellent.

Recent basement finds included lace-trimmed 80 percent silk underwire bras for £7.99, with matching briefs for £4.99. Pure silk and lace-lavished camisoles in white or aqua were £14.99, as were matching tap pants. The half-slips were £25. Ultra-sheer and perfect for summer, pink, yellow, or more opaque white eyelet pure cotton bras were £2.99; matching high-rise panties were £1.40.

Marks & Spencer's skin-care and makeup collec-tions could have filled several suitcases. The Edward-ian Lady skin-care collection is similar to Boots's nat-ural products, down to me-too graphics in the labeling. But Marks & Spencer's products are not only much less expensive, they are packaged in plastic, which makes them safer and lighter to tote than Boots's glass packaging. Especially good are the honey and almond-enriched moisturizer at £1.50 for 100 ml (3½ ounces), aloe vera and apricot moisturizer, also at £1.50 for 100 ml, and a wonderful selection of makeup—for example, a set of eight kohl pencils and a sharpener for £2.99, mascara for £1.25, loose or pressed powder for £1.50, and eye-shadow or lipstick kits for only £2.25.

Let me not forget the men. The best buy in suits is the Italian-designed 100 percent wool suit with two pairs of pants, selling at £90 to £120, praised by many British executive friends.

The Marks & Spencer food department isn't Har-rods, but it isn't bad, either. Even in its selection of breads, which people generally take for granted, Marks & Spencer puts most New York fancy groceries to shame. Cheeses, yogurts, salads, all make quick lunches for shoppers determined not to waste time dining in restaurants.

Reject China

56/57 Beauchamp Place and
33/34/35 Beauchamp Place
    and
183 Brompton Road
London SW3
Tel. (01) 581 0737

134 Regent Street
London W1
Tel. (01) 434 2502

*Mon.–Sat. 9:00–6:00, Sun.
    10:00–6:00 Oct.–May;
Mon.–Sat. 9:00–7:00,
    Sun. 10:00–7:00
    June–Sept.*
*American Express, Diners
    Club, VISA/Barclaycard,
    MasterCard/Access,
    traveler's checks in pounds*
*Mail order; mailing list;
    visits to some U.S. cities in
    fall*

Every year, when I visit England, I find that Reject China has opened at least one new branch. That's one good reason to include it in this book. Reject China sells over 70 percent of its wares to knowledgeable Americans, who can save half to two-thirds off U.S. prices. That's a second good reason to write about the chain.

Reject China started out by selling factory rejects, but for many years now it has sold only first-quality merchandise. It can offer the prices it does because it sells over 80 brands of china, earthenware, crystal, glassware, and silverware, deals in volume, and therefore can afford to work with smaller markups than other shops.

In addition to their usual low prices, there are always specials at Reject China. Not only was Spode's Consul bone china pattern listed at £46 for a five-piece place setting—the same price as two years before—but there was an additional 10 percent off all Spode in stock, which reduced the export price to tourists to only £41.70. A special 50-percent-off sale on Royal Worcester and Spode teapots and coffeepots brought prices down from £21.60–£52.80 to £10.80–£26.40.

Prices on European products are excellent, too. Baccarat, Limoges, and Haviland prices are lower than anywhere except France. Herend prices are lower than anywhere except Hungary. Prices on Waterford crystal are about the same as in Ireland or the Shannon Airport mail-order catalog. Prices on Galway crystal stemware tend to be lower than Shannon's, but the decanters are priced around 25 percent higher.

For selection and overall prices, Reject China is a must-visit. The best time is on Sunday, when nearly all other shops are closed.

Mayfair and Central London

Opportunities Bargain Boutique
119 *New Bond Street*
London W1
Tel. (01) 491 4973

Mon.–Sat. 9:00–6:00
American Express,
  VISA/Barclaycard,
  MasterCard/Access,
  traveler's checks in pounds

Lovers of fine French and European fashion who don't mind wearing the previous season's couture can take advantage of this shop, which features such designers as Nina Ricci and Lanvin at one-third to one-half their original prices.

Yet, even with these reductions, prices are still high. After all, this is couture. Expect to pay £100–£400 for separates, dresses, and suits that were originally as high as £300–£1,200. A Nina Ricci fuchsia silk cocktail dress was marked down from £688 to £240; a Nina Ricci fuchsia silk blouse trimmed with black silk bands, from £214 to £107; and a Lanvin back-buttoned fuchsia and black silk dress, from £472 to £170.

Interestingly, being a small size may be a mixed blessing at Opportunities. When I was there last, there were many separates and ensembles in sizes 14 to 18 that had gone unsold simply because larger women were unaware that designer clothing in their sizes was available to them.

N. Peal   *Mon.–Sat. 9:00–5:30*
37 Burlington Arcade   *American Express,*
London W1   *VISA/Barclaycard,*
Tel. (01) 493 9220   *MasterCard, traveler's*
                                       checks in pounds
                                       Mail order

As faithful readers of *The New Yorker* and *Vogue* magazines know, N. Peal sells thousands of cashmeres a week—to London visitors and through mail order. Most of Peal's merchandise, which is carried in a great variety of color combination and size, is fully priced, as is the merchandise in the majority of shops in the posh, historic Burlington Arcade.

However, there is a wonderful unmarked sale basket in the northern corner of the store that earns N. Peal its bargain rating. This basket, whose contents are always changing, contains sample cashmere sweaters, one-of-a-kinds, the previous year's designs—often small sizes, always wonderful buys. On my last trip, I saw a Pringle gray and peach horizontally striped cardigan with pockets marked down to £39.50. It had no original price tag, but it was probably around £160. Other gems were an emerald green cowl-neck sweater (alas, size 32!) for only £15 and a Valerie Louthan brown, peach, and cream vertically striped reverse-stockinette sweater reduced from £66.50 to £15.

These superbargains rate N. Peal an early visit every time I go to London. If you love cashmere, be sure to plunder their sale basket.

T. Savva
Ladies Hand Made
  Shoemakers
37 Chiltern Street
London W1
Tel. (01) 935 2329

Mon.–Fri. 9:00–5:00, Sat.
  9:00–1:00
Traveler's checks in pounds

Perhaps because it's out of the high-rent district of Jermyn Street and St. James's, this little shop can offer custom-made leather shoes for approximately £65—roughly 20 percent less than the going rate at John Lobb. Boots are around £100.

Savva offers an unusual degree of choice. Rolls of kid and textured leather in a rainbow of colors—teal, russet, mauve, mustard—delight the eye. The store is a must for any woman who is hard to fit, has special orthopedic needs, or simply wants the pleasure of shoes made exactly to measure or the creative joy of designing her own shoes.

Shoes take about two weeks to make. If you're traveling around Britain or Europe, stop here first, order your shoes, and then pick them up on your way home.

South Bank Crafts Centre
South Bank Board
Hungerford Arches—next to
  Royal Festival Hall
London SE1 8XX
Tel. (01) 928 0681

Tues.–Sun. 12:00–7:00
VISA/Barclaycard, traveler's
  checks in pounds
Mail order

The South Bank Crafts Centre, run formerly by the Greater London Council, has a glorious collection of jewelry, ceramics, fabrics, knitwear and weaving, shirts, hats, and accessories. Opened in the fall of 1985, the South Bank Crafts Centre provides a retail outlet to London's most promising young designers. Seventeen artisans are in residence at the center, and visitors can see them at work and even arrange for commissioned work. The following are among the best.

Jewelry

Avril Weston Bartholomew works in metal and in plastics and resins. Her silver jewelry, which starts at £18, uses silver alone or in combination with gold, copper, and/or nickel to create hollow, structured pieces, such as brooches, earrings, and rings. Witty silver earrings resembling a wedge of Swiss cheese cost £25. Hollow silver stud earrings range from £18 to £25. Silver drop earrings are also from £18 to £25; larger ones with a textured surface sell for £30. Domed textured silver earrings with an oxidized surface are priced at £25, and large domed silver crescent-shaped earrings with texture and oxidization, at £40.

Ms. Bartholomew's brooches and rings are equally interesting. A C-shaped silver brooch inlaid with 9-karat gold costs only £35, and a saw-shaped silver and nickel brooch, £60. Other gold-inlaid silver brooches sell for £35–£45, and intricately cut silver and copper brooches, for £60–£80. Highest priced is an intricate prism-shaped silver, nickel, and gold box brooch for £150. Simple, dramatic rings combining silver with 9- or 18-karat gold sell for £38–£40.

Tim Burrows, who also works in silver, says, "When designing and making jewelry, my main concern is decoration, and each piece I make aims to show the material used to the best advantage. I see jewelry as part of the fashion world, and as a result I tend to make extreme decorative pieces." A recent collection of "crumpled" silver earrings featured large round studs for £22.55, large hoops for £27.10, large leaf shapes, also for £27.10, folded and serrated triangle earrings for £30.70, and petal-shaped earrings with a lattice inlay, also for £30.70. His more expensive pieces mix silver with oxidized steel and semiprecious stones.

Gillian Colver is a jeweler, too, but her inspiration comes from historical sources. She says, "I work with a wide variety of materials, both precious and nonprecious, although silver predominates. The shapes I use are simple, usually accompanied by detailed surface decoration known as piercing. Sources which influence my designs include Celtic and Islamic art, art nouveau, and natural forms." In a recent collection of silver pierced fretwork jewelry, earrings decorated with fine silver chains and freshwater pearls sold for £27.10 and £45.10; a coordinating triangular brooch was £37.70.

Joe Richardson, a silversmith whose most recent claim to fame was a commission from the archbishop of Canterbury and Mrs. Runcie for a christening spoon for Prince Harry, says of his work, "I work mainly in gold and silver and enjoy mixing the two metals. I also work with enamels, steel, wood, and shell. Features of my style are clear, simple lines, and I am influenced by Japanese and Egyptian decorative art traditions. I try to avoid large areas of polished metal in my work, as I find that the reflections interfere with the overall design." Richardson's plain silver earrings start at £20. Earrings inlaid with 18-karat gold are £30–£40, while rings inlaid with 18-karat gold start at £45.

Ceramics

Liz Beckenham creates slab-built pots in slender two-dimensional forms that stand approximately 7 inches high. They are decorated with colored glazes, which are incised with linear patterns. Prices start at £22.

Richard Jarman makes domestic pottery in which he uses primary colors to produce a bright, bold effect. His small pitchers are £9.05, and his medium-size ones, £18.05. Small mugs sell for £4.50, and medium-size ones, for £5.40. Small bowls cost £18.05, and the medium-size ones are priced at £21.65. A recent standout was a medium-size bowl with a breezy design of black C-shaped swirls on a bright yellow background for £21.65.

Gina Merrett makes ceramics for everyday use using a potter's wheel. She says, "My work is in red earthenware, mostly thrown. The forms are based on organic shapes—fruits, gourds, etc.—and the painted decoration is influenced by textile designs and by African and other ethnic art. The colors are earthy, based around the colors of natural dyes." A recent collection used a palette of ocher, dark brown, white, and turquoise. Her teapots, coffeepots, and decorative flowerpots start at £18. Mugs start at £3.50, bowls at £5.50, and storage jars at £10.50.

Louise O'Reilly works in white earthenware clay, which is high-biscuit-fired and decorated with colored slips and underglaze color and then painted with a thin glaze. She says, "My ceramic pieces are either press-molded or cast in molds I have made or designed. I work directly onto the mold itself with colored slips and then use a variety of materials to build up pattern and texture on the clay before making the pot itself. After construction, more decoration is added, using slips, stencils, underglaze paints, and crayons. Each piece is then half glazed and finished with wax polish after its final firing. I use these techniques to give an impression of age and fragility to the clay, rather like old wallpaper or eggshell." Prices for her work are quite reasonable, ranging from £10 for a plate to around £100.

Clare Parsons makes domestic stoneware. She says, "I like to make pots people will enjoy using as well as looking at, as I feel function is just as important as form. The basic shape is thrown and then worked on while still wet by altering, cutting, turning, and building to change the symmetry of the form. All my work is decorated with single-color glazes. Architecture and natural forms are the main influences in my work, providing both a traditional sense of balance and order, as well as more fluid, simple forms." Her prices are low. Teapots start at £18, lidded mugs at £7, bowls at £5, cups and saucers at £8, and egg cups at £2.70.

Janice Tchalenko, Britain's leading potter of functional stoneware, has designed a large collection for Dart Pottery in Devon. Prices for this multicolor marble-patterned stoneware start as low as £1.80 for an egg cup and go up to £27 for a large soup tureen. Mugs are £5, a deep bowl is £11, and a teapot costs £18.

Fabric Arts

Janine Berns and Liz Eugene: Maw-Maw Designs. This talented pair has been designing fabric and clothing since 1984, using motifs from African sources. Their fabrics are sold in 3-meter lengths, which are hand-printed bold, abstract prints, designed for either fashion or interiors. Hand-printed silk sells for £25 per meter (£75 per length), and hand-printed cotton, for £16 per meter (£48 per length). Silk shirts cost £55; cotton shirts range from £30 to £45; and accessories, such as bags and scarves, vary between £10 and £20.

Charlie Hackett makes marvelous hand-printed silk scarves, stationery, and textile pictures. He says of his ornately primitive work, "Whilst at the Royal College of Art I created wildly embellished fabrics—jeweled and sequined icons, banners, lengths of glittery silks—all of which sparkled. I am now using the techniques I evolved to create and produce handkerchiefs, greeting cards, writing paper, and other small practical items." His hand-printed silk scarves sell for £27.10. Hand-printed crepe de chine scarves start at £32.50, and the textile pictures, at £60. Hand-printed stationery can be bought for as low as 50p.

Katherine Hyde is a weaver. She says, "Using a simple table loom, I create complex designs by adding a number of colored threads into each row. The selvage edges of my scarves have an intrinsic part to play in the design, and their heavy patterning is a result of the brocading technique, which has been used for thousands of years by ancient cultures throughout the world. It is these cultures that have inspired many of my designs. In order to make my work more accessible to more people, I have started making up my weaving into small purses, bags, and hats." This art is certainly affordable now. Her hats start at £27, with silk hats beginning at £36.10. Purses range from £3.60 to £7.20, while scarves vary from £35 to £47.

Lindsay Keir has exhibited in Paris and all over Scotland. Her highly decorated hand-painted silk hats and silk cushions start at £40, her hand-painted silk pictures at £50, and her hand-painted silk embroideries at £150. By the time you read this, her first collection of silk clothes and accessories may be at the South Bank Crafts Centre.

Lindy Richardson does brightly colored primitive-looking designs. Her hand-printed handkerchiefs are £5.40 in cotton and £18 in silk. Her textile and beaded jewelry sells for £20.70–£27.60, and her miniature embroideries and tapestries start at £36.70.

CHELSEA

Alison Robson
By appointment only
Fashion & Knitwear Designer   *Traveler's checks in pounds*
4 Smith Street
London SW3
Tel. (01) 730 3768

This talented young designer, whose hand-knitted goods are carried by Saks Fifth Avenue and Macy's in the United States and by Joseph of Tricot fame, Top Spin, and Scottish Merchant in Covent Garden in London, sells her samples and stock from previous seasons to private customers at wholesale prices.

Alison does knitwear in natural fibers—wool, cotton, and silk—imparting a high-fashion twist to English tradition. Her bold, pretty designs cost £40–£100 in wool or cotton and £80–£200 in silk. Aran patchwork sweater-dresses are priced at £80–£90, silk dresses at £140–£150, and silk skirts at £80.

To complete the high-fashion look, there are matching or coordinating machine-knit accessories, such as stockings for £14, and hats at around £10.

Alison will also work to order in about the same price range.

"Sava" Fashions

5 Beauchamp Place
London SW3
Tel. (01) 581 1931

Mon.–Sat. 9:30–6:00
American Express,
*   VISA/Barclaycard,*
*   MasterCard/Access,*
*   traveler's checks*

Où sont les coutures d'antan? With apologies to François Villon, Sava's basement holds the answer. Skip the small ground-floor area, which has no bargains, and head downstairs immediately.

Original prices aren't usually indicated, and price tags are on hard-to-get-to hemlines, but these are minor quibbles. The prices and amenities compensate. You can pick up Balmain emerald or white silk dresses with black polka dots for £195, a navy cashmere suit for only £150, and a brown tweed suit with a rust leather collar for £195. Says owner Robert Harris, "Other than Balmain and some other major names, many of our French, Italian, and German designers are not well known and are exclusive to our shop. If we can't sell the designs in three to four weeks, we keep marking them down."

In the summer, Sava opens its garden, where gentlemen are served coffee while their ladies shop and try on clothes for their approval.

Outer London

Prue Bowyer
33 Albany Road
London W13
Tel. (01) 998 7095

By appointment
Cash only

Prue Bowyer is a very sophisticated clean-cut designer, inspired by the details of men's tailoring. She sells to the Italian market, so you know she must be good. And she sells samples and stock from previous seasons to private customers at wholesale prices.

Her silhouettes are similar to those of Giorgio Armani and Basile—classic, with interesting details, like godets in back of coats, and turned-up, contrasting coat collars.

In separates, Prue coordinates dresses, jackets, pants, skirts, and coats in wool crepes and jacquard prints, used on the wrong side for an abstract effect. Wholesale prices range from around £30 for pants and skirts to around £130 for coats.

David Evans & Co.
Silk Printers, Dyers and
   Finishers
Bourne Park Industrial Estate
Bourne Road
Crayford, Kent DA1 4BP
Tel. (0322) 57521

Mon.–Fri. 10:30–4:30, Sat.
   9:00–12:30
VISA/Barclaycard,
   MasterCard/Access,
   traveler's checks in pounds

The town of Crayford, on the Greater London–Kent border, has only one notable factory shop. If you're looking for designer scarves by Liberty, Charvet of Paris, or Hermès, silk ties, and silk by the meter, take the forty-minute train trip from London. It's so satisfying to have bought a Liberty scarf here for £6.99 and then see the same one at Heathrow Airport's duty-free shop for £29.99!

Since 1825, David Evans has been printing beautiful silk fabrics, and it is now the only company still able to produce the famous ancient madder silk beloved by designers, from Gloria Sachs and Ralph Lauren to Sulka and Brooks Brothers.

If you sew or have a dressmaker, you must visit the David Evans mill shop. David Evans has the most sumptuous collection of silk fabrics I have ever seen—from featherweight crepe de chine to heavy silk twill, both in solids and in beautiful patterns. Widths range from 36 to 54 inches, and prices are only £4 per meter for plain dyed silks and £6 per meter for printed silks, which is approximately one-third the U.S. price.

Especially pretty are a dark blue silk twill, perfect for a summer jacket or blazer, at £4 per meter, and a small, muted paisley print in blue and red on navy crepe de chine, a tiny blue and gray foulard pattern in blue and gray on wine, a small peach and blue foulard pattern on teal silk twill, and a small teal and violet pattern on a lighter-weight dusty rose silk twill—all at £6 per meter.

Even more unusual, and a wonderful bargain, is David Evans's 40-inch-wide printed cashmere for only £35 per meter. A bold foulard pattern in pale yellow, tobacco, and red with black and white accents is perfect for the most luxurious shirtwaist dress, shirt, skirt, bathrobe, pajamas, or nightgown.

Cotton curtain fabric by the posh London decorating firm Colefax & Fowler was only £1 per meter here, and probably at least £10 per meter in Mayfair, at Colefax & Fowler's posh showroom.

There are also bins of wonderful remnants for as low as 50p.

If you don't sew, visit David Evans for early Christmas presents. Men's and women's silk handkerchiefs are only £1 each—buy them by the dozen. Silk ties are £5 and £6 here and up to £20 in London's department stores. Square silk scarves measuring 27, 30, 33, and 36 inches start at £4, and oblong silk scarves measuring 30 by 9 inches to 48 by 9 inches, at £5.

Wool shawls are a great bargain, too—£17.50 for a 54-inch square here and around £40 in London.

For the little girls on your list, or maybe even for yourself, David Evans makes lovely rag dolls for only £8.50 that wear silk dresses and pantalettes made of Evans fabrics.

Chapter 5 *Stoke-on-Trent/ Staffordshire*

Is it worth running up to Stoke-on-Trent for the day? Absolutely, if you love to shop for china and pottery. Stoke-on-Trent is England's china-manufacturing capital, and there are over a dozen factory outlets to delight you.

British Rail makes it easy. Trains leave from London's Euston Station and whisk you up to Stoke-on-Trent in just under two hours. To enjoy a full day's shopping, here are some trains to take. As in continental Europe, the timetable is on a 24-hour clock, where 1:00 A.M. is written as 0100, and 1:00 P.M., as 1300. Remember to check with British Rail the day before to confirm that the timetable below is still in effect.

London Euston dep.	(Mon.-Sat.) Stoke-on-Trent arr.	Stoke-on-Trent dep.	London Euston arr.
0815	1010	1412	1615
0950	1149	1647	1844

Bull in a China Shop

Lichfield Street
Hanley
Stoke-on-Trent
Staffordshire ST1 3EB
Tel. (0782) 263934

Mon.–Sat. 10:00–5:15
American Express,
VISA/Barclaycard,
MasterCard/Access,
traveler's checks in pounds

This factory outlet carries pottery, earthenware, and cookware from the Wedgwood subsidiaries Johnson Brothers, J & G Meakin, Midwinter, and William Adams. Table linen and crystal come in occasionally, too.

The prices are excellent. In Asiatic Pheasant, a canceled export order available in dark pink or blue, dinner plates were £1.40, coffeepots were £8.15, and the covered vegetable dish was £7.80.

In the Jamestown Hearts and Flowers pattern, which resembles French Quimper ware, a naïf country pattern, dinner plates were £1.50, the jumbo cup was £1.70, and the matching saucer was £1.15.

Franciscan's Desert Rose or Fresh Fruit dinner plates were priced at £1.90, cereal bowls at £1, cups at £1.15, and saucers at 75p. Midwinter's oven to tableware Invitation pattern of pink carnations is perfect for microwave. Dinner plates sold for £2.14, cereal bowls for £1.20, soup bowls for £1.85, cups for £1.14, and saucers for 62p. Casseroles ranged from £4.30 to £7.55.

Other casserole dishes, featured in the shop's bargain basement, came in decorator colors of brown, rust, blue, and mustard and cost only £2.50.

The shop's only negative is its lack of shipping facilities, common to many factory outlets. It will pack your purchases, but you must take them to the post office or carry them home.

Coalport Gift Shop

King Street
Fenton
Stoke-on-Trent
Staffordshire ST4 3JB
Tel. (0782) 49174

Mon.–Thurs. 9:30–4:30,
Fri. 9:30–3:30, Sat.
10:00–5:00
American Express,
VISA/Barclaycard,
MasterCard/Access,
traveler's checks in pounds

Coalport china, decorative plates, figurines, and accessories that have been discontinued or are slightly imperfect are sold here. The selection is quite varied and changes every week. The key to pricing and bargains is the color in which the prices are written: red ink means that the items are specially priced or discontinued and have been marked down 50 percent; blue or black ink means that items are slightly imperfect and are marked down 27½ percent.

Two dinner plates in Cairo, a long-discontinued wine-colored pattern embellished with great quantities of gold, were only £35 each and would make a lovely breakfront display. Decorative plates ranged from cobalt-and-gold-bordered scenes of historic buildings or paintings of flowers for £24.95 to a reproduction of Renoir's *Oarsmen at Chatou,* made for the National Gallery of Arts in Washington, D.C., for £7.50.

In dinnerware, a 29-piece service in Indian Tree Coral was £293.25. Hunting Scene, whose pieces are usually sold separately, offered some pieces at an additional 20 percent discount on top of the 27½ percent discount simply because they were backstamped "Crown Staffordshire," a discontinued label. (Now it's all marked "Coalport.") That reduced prices of dinner plates to £7.60.

Cake plates and matching servers cost £19.90–£22.45, depending on the pattern, and make excellent gifts. For stocking stuffers, pomanders at £1.50, china flower brooches at £2.00–£4.95, and china flower earrings at £2.50 make great buys.

Mason's Ironstone
Broad Street
Hanley
Stoke-on-Trent
Staffordshire ST1 4HH
Tel. (0782) 264354

Mon.–Sat. 10:00–4:00
VISA/Barclaycard,
MasterCard/Access,
traveler's checks in pounds

This factory shop has the most interesting odds and ends, with the best prices in all of Stoke-on-Trent.

Savings run from 35 to over 75 percent. However, your best attitude and shopping strategy here is to buy individual pieces for yourself or as gifts. You probably won't find a service for eight at this shop.

Mason's ironstone, much of it decorated with 22K gold, has been manufactured for nearly 200 years. Mandalay, the top-selling pattern of the group, has a ginger jar that sells for £35.90 here and £59 at retail. Regency, a pattern called Plantation Colonial in the United States, where it was first imported in 1880, had some unusual bargains: one jumbo cup and saucer for £4.65, two sets for £7.95, a savings of £1.35 on the factory-outlet price. Dinner plates were £2.30, and salad plates, £1.50.

Yellow Flowers, a pattern made for Tiffany, was only £1.50 for the salad plates—but salad plates were the only pieces that were available. There was only one sample cachepot in that pattern: a superb buy at £5. Soap dishes made for Crabtree & Evelyn were 85p.

The charming fluted Blue Denmark dinner plates were £1.20, and the salad plates, 70p.

Christmas Village, a far more attractive and visually interesting pattern than Spode's Christmas Tree, is here now, too, at less than half the British retail price, and probably between 25 and 33 percent of the U.S. retail price. So far, the soufflé dishes (£1.90–£4.20) and large serving bowls (£11.98) outnumber giftware, such as candlesticks, mugs, and cake stands, but new stock is coming in all the time.

Minton China
London Road
Stoke-on-Trent ST4 7QD
Tel. (0782) 49171

Mon.–Fri. 9:00–4:30; closed
factory holidays
American Express, Diners
Club, VISA/Barclaycard,
MasterCard/Access,
traveler's checks in pounds
Will ship first-quality
merchandise only

Minton's factory shop has two parts: one sells first-quality pieces at the full retail price; the other sells slight seconds and discontinued patterns at lower prices, sometimes at well over 50 percent off the original price.

Dinner plates were the star bargains of a recent visit. Saturn, a pattern with a crimson, turquoise, or cobalt rim, was priced at £3.95, and the Bellemead pattern, at £4.95. Persian Rose, Marquesa, Grasmere, St. James, Avonlea, Stanwood, and Grosvenor plates were all £6.95 each. The most expensive sale plate, at £12.95, was Buckingham, which has a very heavy and ornate gold rim.

Another good buy was the Royal Kent 18-piece tea set, with peach or pink poppies and gray leaves on a white background, for only £14.95. Assorted one- and few-of-a-kind teapots were £7.95, and coffeepots, £6.95.

Portmeirion Potteries Ltd.

563 King Street
Longton
Stoke-on-Trent ST3 1EZ
Tel. (0782) 326412

Mon.–Wed. 8:30–4:00,
Thurs. 8:30–3:00, Fri.
8:30–3:30, Sat.
9:30–12:30
American Express,
VISA/Barclaycard,
MasterCard/Access,
traveler's checks in pounds
Mail order

This is the largest of Portmeirion's four factory shops; however, the shop in Newcastle, Staffordshire and the shop in Stafford have longer weekday and Saturday hours.

Portmeirion makes a number of patterns dear to any Audubon lover's heart—especially Birds of Britain, Fish, and Botanical Garden—with a different species of flora or fauna and its scientific name on each plate, bowl, or baking dish. There is no gold on any of the pieces, so they are perfect for microwave cooking and are dishwasher safe.

Prices are so low, even compared to London's Reject China, to say nothing of New York, that it pays to buy as much as you like, even though shipping can double your purchase price. (You'd have to pay shipping from London, too.)

In the Birds of Britain pattern, a large oval Mute Swan serving platter was only £5.35, the 16-inch oval baking dish was £9.25, and the 12-inch quiche pan was £7.75. The 10-inch quiche pan in a number of designs from Botanical Garden or Birds of Britain was priced at £5.80, and the 10-by 12½-inch lasagna pan in designs from Botanical Garden or Fish was £8.35. In the Summer Strawberry pattern, the 4-pint casserole cost £13.50, and the 6-pint casserole, £16.50. The 10-inch dinner plate in designs from Botanical Garden, Birds of Britain, or Fish was only £2.75, and the gigantic salad bowl, £11.65. Large breakfast cups and saucers in many patterns were £3.05.

Botanical Garden vases were great buys, in sizes of 5 inches (£2.30), 7 inches (£3.25), 9 inches (£4.20), and 11 inches (£5.85). Flowerpots in Botanical Garden or Summer Strawberry ranged from a 3-inch pot for £1.95 to an 8¼-inch pot for £7.65.

Portmeirion's solid crimson Red Dragon cookware was reduced 50 percent, with the oval baking dish marked down from £6.60 to £3.30, the 6-inch soufflé dish from £4.75 to £2.37, and the 7-inch soufflé dish from £5.70 to £2.85.

Portmeirion Potteries Ltd.
167 London Road
Stoke-on-Trent ST4 7QE
Tel. (0782) 411756

Mon.–Wed. 8:30–4:00,
Thurs. 8:30–3:00, Fri.
8:30–3:30, Sat.
9:30–12:30
American Express,
VISA/Barclaycard,
MasterCard/Access,
traveler's checks in pounds
Mail order

This is one of Portmeirion's four branches, all located close to one another in Staffordshire. If one branch doesn't have the piece you are looking for, ask the salesperson to phone the other branches and have the piece held for you until you can get over there. Note that the shops all have different hours, with the shop in Newcastle, Staffordshire and the shop in Stafford (see below) having the longest weekday and Saturday hours.

See p. 53 for a complete write-up of Portmeirion's largest factory shop, located in Longton.

Portmeirion Potteries Ltd.
25 George Street
Newcastle-under-Lyme
    Staffordshire ST4 2JS
Tel. (0782) 615192

Mon.–Wed., Fri 9:30–5:00,
    Sat. 9:30–4:00; closed
    Thurs.
American Express,
    VISA/Barclaycard,
    MasterCard/Access,
    traveler's checks in pounds
Mail order

Of the four branches of Portmeirion Potteries, all located close to one another in Staffordshire, this branch and the branch in Stafford (see below) have the best shopping hours.

See p. 53 for a complete write-up of Portmeirion's largest factory shop, located in Longton.

Portmeirion Potteries Ltd.
56a Gaol Street
Stafford ST16 2NR
Tel. (0785) 40353

Mon.–Tues., Thurs.–Sat.
    9:30–5:00;
American Express,
    VISA/Barclaycard,
    MasterCard/Access,
    traveler's checks in pounds
Mail order

Of the four branches of Portmeirion Potteries, all located close to one another in Staffordshire, this branch and the branch in Newcastle (see p. 55) have the longest shopping hours.

See p. 53 for a complete write-up of Portmeirion's largest factory shop, located in Longton.

Royal Doulton

Nile Street
Burslem
Stoke-on-Trent ST6 2AJ
Tel. (0782) 85747
7 4 4 7 6 6

Mon.–Fri. 9:00–4:30
American Express, Diners
Club, VISA/Barclaycard,
MasterCard/Access,
traveler's checks in pounds
Will ship first-quality
merchandise only

Like Minton (see p. 52), its sister shop, the Royal Doulton factory shop is divided into two parts: one carries perfect merchandise at full retail prices; the other half carries slight seconds, discontinued patterns, and odds and ends. Don't come here for a full dinner service, but do come here to buy unusual pieces, an interesting service for one or two, or a delightful assortment of cups and saucers.

On a recent trip, I found long-spouted bone china teapots for only £7.95 and short-spouted teapots for £5.60. Coffeepots were £6.75. In Carlyle, a pretty pattern with a teal-green and gold border decorated with blue flowers, cups and saucers were £7.95, and creamers, £3.75. No other pieces were available. Vanborough, an elegant pattern in leather green and lots of gold, had creamers and covered sugar bowls for £3.75 each and saucers for only 95p. Unfortunately, there were no cups —doubly unfortunate because cups are broken much more frequently than saucers. Odd cups were 65p, and odd saucers, 50p. Sometimes they matched or coordinated. Assorted dinner plates ranged from £2.45 to £10.45.

Whiteware bone china was very inexpensive, and there was enough to assemble many sets. Plates were

90p for the 10-inch size, 60p for the 9-inch, 55p for the 8-inch, and 50p for the 6-inch. Cups and saucers were £1.45 for the smaller size and £1.60 for the larger one. Coffeepots and teapots were £3.35 each, and the cream soup and stand, only £1.10.

Spode "Seconds" Shop

Church Street
Stoke-on-Trent ST4 1BX
Tel. (0782) 46011

Mon.–Thurs. 8:30–5:00,
Fri. 8:30–4:00, Sat.
10:00–4:00; closed bank
holidays
VISA/Barclaycard,
MasterCard/Access,
traveler's checks in pounds
Mail order

Spode's "Seconds" Shop carries very slight seconds and discontinued patterns in dinner, tea, and coffee services, and giftware in Spode's bone china, earthenware, and stoneware. Occasionally Royal Worcester products are available here, too, but for a much wider selection, visit the Royal Worcester factory shop in Worcester (see p. 108). Savings compared to British retail prices vary, but start at 33 percent. During the three- to four-week semiannual sales beginning in mid-July and right after Christmas, prices are marked down even more.

On a recent visit, Spode's Blue Italian, a famous earthenware pattern that has been in continuous production since 1816, was marked down 50 percent. A soufflé dish was reduced from £17 to £8.50, a covered oval vegetable dish from £20.95 to £10.50, and a covered round vegetable dish from £22.95 to £11.50. Ginger jars that could double as lamps were only £20, and large canisters were marked down to £10.

In Trade Winds, a stone china pattern of clipper ships available in blue, black, or coral red, dinner plates were reduced from £14.25 to £8.10, and the large breakfast cup and saucer were marked down from £20.05 to £11.40.

In Consul Cobalt, a simple, elegant bone china pattern, most reductions were only 25 percent, but an 18-piece tea set was a bargain at 50 percent off: from £87.60 to £43.80. The Noah's Ark nursery pattern was also on sale: the cereal bowl was £2.55, the plate was £2.70, and the bank (called a money box) was £5.35.

Bowpot, a discontinued chinoiserie pattern in blues and coral, was an enormous bargain, marked down 75 percent. Dinner plates were reduced from £13 to £3.25, the cream soup from £12.20 to £3.05, the large breakfast cup and saucer from £18.20 to £4.55, the smaller dinner cup and saucer from £12.20 to £3.05, the coffeepot from £44.95 to £11.25, the covered vegetable dish from £65.30 to £16.35, and the salt and pepper shakers from £6.65 each to only £1.65 each.

During sale periods, the Spode Shop also carries items made by Royal Worcester, its sister company (see p. 108). Best buys include the popular Evesham (harvest fruit) soufflé dishes, marked down 50 percent. The large size is reduced from £13.10 to £6.55, the medium size from £10.45 to £5.25, and the small size from £9.40 to £4.70.

Staffordshire Enamels Ltd.

Mon.–Fri. 9:30–3:00
Cash only

Cinderhill Industrial Estate
Weston Coyney Road
Longton
Stoke-on-Trent ST3 5JT
Tel. (0782) 322948

If you love enameled boxes, make sure to visit Staffordshire Enamels, and bring lots of cash. To my regret, I was low on cash (but high on credit cards) by the time I visited the factory shop, and I had to forgo three or four pieces that I still wish I had bought.

The pieces available are all samples, discontinued designs, and slight seconds; but if you choose carefully from the last group, the tiny imperfections will be virtually invisible.

The designs here are more varied than those of Halcyon Days, which is better known to Americans, and the prices are a fraction of that competitor's, with the largest and most expensive box here costing a mere £15. In this top group of masterpieces of miniature painting—the boxes are only 2½ inches in diameter— were the Granada box, an elaborate William Morris pattern in orange, yellow, and tobacco brown, lavished with 22-karat gold, and the Statue of Liberty box, the only centennial souvenir with any style and grace, which I saw at a posh shop on 57th Street in Manhattan for $125. Among the large round boxes were one showing a pair of playful raccoons, one of mallards, and one of a rainbow trout surrounded by a tackle box and fishing flies.

There was a large group of medium-size round boxes for £12, including floral designs, a clever-looking Siamese, and a collection based on the charming illustrations in *The Country Diary of an Edwardian Lady,* a bestseller several years ago. Oval boxes, also for £12, include such London landmarks as St. Paul's Cathedral and the Houses of Parliament.

Small round and oval boxes cost only £9. Some of the prettiest had floral patterns, like wild roses (called dog roses), wild pansies, bluebells, primroses, and poppies. Other charmers had mottoes within floral borders, like their predecessors, the 18th-century Bilston trinket boxes: "Thank You," "With Love," "With Fond Wishes," "For You," "Love and Be Happy," and many other tender sentiments. A group of beautifully painted boxes with fruit motifs—strawberries, blackberries, gooseberries, raspberries, black cherries, or a single succulent peach—were also £9.

Miniature boxes with teddy bears playing golf, cricket, or tennis, ice skating, riding on a rocking horse, playing Santa Claus, or wearing a skirt, pajamas, bow tie, or scarf cost £5 (screwtop lids) or £7 (hinged lids). These make wonderful gifts.

Egg-shaped boxes were £12 and came in wonderful designs of circus seals, a hot-air balloon, lilies of the valley, and butterflies alighting on flowers on a pale yellow background.

Probably the most useful boxes are the pillboxes and stamp boxes—£12 for the medium size and £15 for the large size. A parade of penguins came as both pillbox and stamp box for £15, as did a group of steeplechase horse racers. A Mercator projection map of the world comes in both versions for £12 each.

Wedgwood Visitor Centre

Barlaston
Stoke-on-Trent
Staffordshire ST12 9ES
Tel. (078 139) 4218 or 4141

Main shop: Mon.–Fri. 9:00–5:00, Sat. 10:00–4:00
Seconds shop: Mon.–Fri. 9:00–5:00, Sat. in Mar.–Dec. 10:00–4:00
American Express, Diners Club, VISA/Barclaycard, MasterCard/Access, traveler's checks in pounds, foreign currency

Most products are full price because Wedgwood believes in protecting its retailers. However, occasionally there are discontinued designs or colors or slightly imperfect items, especially in Wedgwood jasperware jewelry. Pendants were £6.45 to £6.95 (£14.25 if perfect), and rings were £6 and £9.80 (£18–£22 if perfect).

Of far greater interest is Wedgwood's seconds shop, the home of slightly imperfect, discontinued, and sample products made by all the companies of the Wedgwood group: Wedgwood Crystal, Dartington Glass, Coalport China, Mason's Ironstone, William Adams, Johnson Brothers, J & G Meakin, Midwinter, and Crown Staffordshire. Visit this shop even if you plan to visit the separate subsidiaries' factory shops because the merchandise varies so greatly. Sample bargains, although stock changes very rapidly, include a Wedgwood small teal jasperware vase for £8.60 (£14.95 if perfect), a teal jasperware heart-shaped box for £8.80 (£14.35 if perfect), Wedgwood Crystal bird paperweights for £6.95, and an admiral decanter for £70.50.

Note: There is a £50 minimum for reclaiming the VAT and a £1 admission charge to the Visitor Centre —well worth it to see the craftsmen at work and the renowned museum.

BURTON-ON-TRENT

Georgian Crystal (Tutbury) Ltd.
Silk Mill Lane
Tutbury
Near Burton-on-Trent
Staffordshire DE13 9NG
Tel. (0283) 814534

Mon.–Sat. 9:00–5:00
American Express, Diners
*   Club, VISA/Barclaycard,*
*   MasterCard/Access,*
*   traveler's checks in pounds*
Mail order

Burton-on-Trent isn't far from Stoke-on-Trent, so serious shoppers may be able to get their crystal as well as their china all in one day's outing.

Prices at Georgian Crystal's factory shop are about half the prices of similar lead crystal in London. Liqueur glasses are £3.63–£4.25, depending on the pattern. Large 9-ounce rummers (similar to old-fashioned tumblers) are £4.75–£5.50. Decanters range from £37 to £56, depending on the pattern and shape, including ship's decanters (£55 and £56).

Small items are really a bargain here. Violet vases are only £3.50, and bud vases start at £4. Elegant little candlesticks are £6 each, a honey jar with lid is £7, and a sugar and creamer set is £14. Flower vases range from £5 to £35 as they rise from 4 inches to 10 inches.

Bonus: Visitors are welcome to watch the glass-blowing, cutting, and engraving.

Tutbury Crystal

Burton Street
Tutbury
Near Burton-on-Trent
Staffordshire DE13 9NG
Tel. (0283) 813281

Mon.–Sat. 9:00–5:00
VISA/Barclaycard,
MasterCard/Access,
traveler's checks in pounds
Mail order

Tutbury Crystal sells primarily to retail shops throughout Britain, but its factory shop sells slight seconds to the public.

Prices at Tutbury Crystal's factory shop, like those of its neighbor, Georgian Crystal, are around half the London prices. Liqueur glasses range from £3.63 to £4.59, depending on the pattern. Tutbury, which has a greater merchandise range than Georgian, offers both 10-ounce rummers (with a squarer shape) and 10-ounce old-fashioned glasses. The rummers are slightly more expensive than the old-fashioned glasses (£4.91–£5.80 versus £4.27–£5.04). Decanters are well priced, too, ranging from £24.86 to £41.18, the most expensive ship's decanter.

Small gift items are a buy here. Violet vases in three patterns range from £4.65 to £5.04, and ten varieties of bud vases, from £3.63 to £7.20. There are 21 other vase patterns, priced at £4.59 to £30.35. Low candlesticks are £5.67; taller, more graceful ones are £6.38. Covered honey jars cost £7.14 and £7.46, while covered honey churns—a slightly different shape—run £8.03 and £8.86. A sugar and creamer set is £16.38. Paperweights are £7.01 and £8.48.

Chapter 6 *Nottingham*

Nottingham is a wonderful shopper's day trip from London. For us demon shoppers, it's not Robin Hood and the sheriff of Nottingham that enthrall us, but rather the factory outlets of Elbeo, Viyella, and all the lace and knitwear outlets.

Here is the timetable from London's St. Pancras Station, shown, as customary in Europe, on a 24-hour clock, where 1:00 A.M. is written as 0100, and 1:00 P.M., as 1300. The trip to Nottingham takes just under two hours. As always, remember to check with British Rail to make sure that this timetable is still in effect.

London St. Pancras dep.	(Mon.-Sat.) Nottingham arr.	Nottingham dep.	London St. Pancras arr.
0700	0900	1500	1656
0820	1012	1605	1800
0910	1055	1658	1842

NOTTINGHAM CITY

Goosefayre
46 Friar Lane
Nottingham NG1
Tel. (0602) 413713

Mon.–Sat. 9:30–5:30
Diners Club,
VISA/Barclaycard,
MasterCard/Access

Don't let the arch name or spelling put you off—until the lace factories open their doors to private cus-

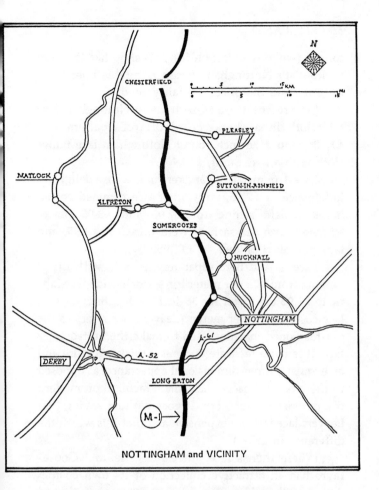

NOTTINGHAM and VICINITY

The wonderful highways in and around Nottingham make it easy to do all your shopping in a day.

tomers (we're working on it!), this shop has the only nontouristy Nottingham cotton lace table linens and lingerie. And the prices are fairly good.

On a recent trip, a 54-inch square Nottingham lace tablecloth in a checkerboard of roses pattern was £16.80, and a 56-inch round Nottingham lace tablecloth with a rose motif, £19.90.

Lace-trimmed silk handkerchiefs were a delightful indulgence at £7.95, with other lace-trimmed cotton handkerchiefs selling for £2.95 and £3.95. Lace-trimmed lavender sachets were priced at £3.95, and lacy potpourri pillows, at £11.95.

Lace is sold here separately as well, with prices ranging from 90p per meter for ¼-inch-wide lace fabric to £1.95 per meter for 36-inch-wide fabric. Leavers lace costs £1–£5 per meter. (Leavers lace refers to the old-fashioned machine used to make the best-quality lace. It is more intricate and has a thicker texture and an exquisite three-dimensional appearance, as opposed to the modern Raschel lace, manufactured on modern computerized machinery. It goes without saying that Leavers lace is more expensive and that it is worth the difference in price.)

Where there's lace, there's lingerie, and Goosefayre has an attractive collection of its own custom designs. Silk and lace camisoles are £25; sets of silk and lace camisoles with matching tap pants are £50. Most luxurious, but a real extravagance—yet priced reasonably compared to what Saks or Bloomingdale's would charge—is a pale pink silk nightgown for £125, with exquisite lace cascading over the front of the bodice and down the sides of the gown to the waist. The matching peignoir, also festooned with lace, is £75.

Liz Nelson Studios Ltd

11/15 Heathcote Street
Nottingham NG1 3AF
Tel. (062) 410696

By appointment
Traveler's checks in pounds
Mail order

Liz Nelson is a designer who specializes in leather and suede couture. You can buy her samples by appointment, at below-wholesale prices.

A hot-orange suede jacket with nipped-in waist was priced at £119. The matching pants were £98, and the matching skirt was £78. Her textured suede over-sized jacket with peplum and belt in fuchsia, black, or beige was £119, and its matching skirt, £79. Handbags ran £15–£20; belts, around £10; and hats, a very low £15.

Liz Nelson's leather and suede evening designs are knockouts. A black suede evening top with Cleopatra beaded collar had three variations: sleeveless, £80; with peplum, £109; and with sleeves and beaded cuffs, £149.

The greatest bargains are found on a rack with samples from previous seasons. An aqua suede top with leather trim, originally £90 wholesale, was marked down to £59. A fuchsia padded leather jacket, originally £140 wholesale, was now only £100. A fuchsia suede blouse with pleated bodice was £59, and a similar black suede cocktail dress, only £100.

ALFRETON

David Nieper Ltd.
Nottingham Road
Alfreton
Derbyshire DE5 7XA
Tel. (0773) 833335

Mon.–Fri. 10:30–3:30,
occasional Sat. (phone first)
Cash only
Mail order at retail prices
through catalog from
Saulgrove House,
Long Sutton, Basingstoke,
Hampshire RG25 1SR.
(0773) 836000 (too expensive
to be recommended)

Lovers of luxury lingerie, look no farther! If you've become disheartened by the rising cost of exquisite lingerie, and the near impossibility of finding pure silk or cotton smalls, as the British call them, for less than $50–$60 or nightgowns for less than $150, take heart. The David Nieper factory shop makes them affordable once more.

Nieper's merchandise, designed at the factory, includes nightgowns, negligees, teddies (called camiknickers), pajamas, robes, full and half slips, camisoles, tap pants (called French knickers), panties, briefs, and bras—all in silks, cottons, and polyester satins and blends. As a sybarite, I'll stick to the silks and cottons. The other merchandise is as lovely, but just doesn't feel the same on the skin.

Best buys are the discontinued lines, ends of lines, slight seconds, and sample garments, which sell at a 50-percent discount from the catalog prices. Perfect current styles are discounted 30–35 percent.

Nieper's designs bespeak pure luxury. They are characterized by elegant pintucking details and slathers of pure cotton Nottingham Leavers lace.

Quoted here are prices for the previous season's styles, which were 50 percent less than the usual retail prices. A silk and lace nightgown in ivory or pale green was £61; a full slip in the same colors, £42.50; and a silk and lace camisole top and matching tap pants in those colors, £27.50 each. A hard-to-find silk and lace garter belt (called suspender belt), again in ivory or pale green, was only £9.25.

David Nieper does a collection similar to that of Hanro of Switzerland but at much more reasonable prices. The pure Sea Islands cotton is knitted, dyed, and finished in Switzerland, then made into garments trimmed with pure cotton Leavers lace at the Nieper factory. The teddy in cream or white is £9.75, the matching camisole £5.75, and the V-neck top £8. The briefs are £4.50, and the tap pants, £7.50.

For summer, Nieper does lightweight cotton lingerie using broderie anglaise, a charming embroidered fabric. In a summery white, the bra is £7.25, the briefs are £5, and the garter belt is £6.75.

One great advantage of David Nieper's superb lingerie is that it comes in large sizes. Women who wear a 38D bra or a size 18/20 dress can enjoy the same sensual underwear and lingerie as their size 6, 34B sisters. I wish American lingerie designers would learn that lesson!

DERBY

Royal Crown Derby
194 Osmaston Road
Derby DE3 8J2
Tel. (0332) 47051

Mon.–Fri. 9:15–4:15; closed Whit week (seventh week after Easter), holidays, and Christmas week

American Express, Diners Club, VISA/Barclaycard, MasterCard/Access

Royal Crown Derby's discounts don't seem as high as those offered by its competitors in Stoke-on-Trent (see pp. 49–63), but if you love their patterns, this is the place to buy them. The factory shop does offer some good buys in odds and ends.

Crown Derby's bone china creatures patterned in blue, navy, and coral and lavished with gold are among the very few figurines I find attractive—perhaps because the artists have captured the essence of the animal's personality. The fox, harvest mouse, rabbit, and wren sell for £18.30 if slightly imperfect, and for £27.50 if perfect. The quail, duck, hedgehog, owl, penguin, pig, and snail are priced at £22 if slightly imperfect, and at £33 if perfect. The pheasant, turtle, frog, seal, and cat cost £26 if slightly imperfect and £39 if perfect.

Imperia, an obsolete pattern with an elaborate turquoise and gold rim, offered good buys. The fruit/ cereal bowls were £5, and the cups and saucers, £8. The coffeepot was priced at £25, the covered sugar bowl at £15, and the sauceboat at £10. The crescent-shaped salad plates were £10, and the soup tureen was £35. If only there had been dinner plates!

Red Aves, one of my favorite patterns, had a number of slight seconds, marked down one-third. The dinner plates were £10.65, the fluted luncheon plates £14.35, the fruit/cereal bowls £9.65, the crescent-shaped salad plates £16.35, the bread and butter plates £4.85, and the cups and saucers £10.35. The creamer was priced at £11.95.

Brittany, a pretty pattern of cherries and lacy fuchsia ovals, had only cups and saucers—but they were a good buy reduced from £10.35 to £4.95—and there was a large collection of coffeepots marked down from £63.65 to £29.95.

HUCKNALL

William Hollins "Viyella"

Caddaw Avenue
Hucknall NG 15 7JR
Tel. (0602) 632121

Tues.–Fri. 9:30–12:00 and
2:00–4:30, Sat.
9:00–12:30; closed Whit
week (seventh week after
Easter) and Christmas week
Cash only

I haven't omitted visiting Viyella's sister shop—it's the Jaeger knitwear shop marked "Ewe"—three blocks away. After a quick run through the racks, I decided that it didn't rate a write-up.

William Hollins "Viyella" carries an interesting mixture of clothes and accessories for men, women, and children, as well as cotton flannel sheets and curtain fabric.

True to its name, much of the shop's merchandise is made of Viyella, a luxury blend of 55 percent wool and 45 percent cotton. The prices are excellent. Viyella blouses in dark floral prints or with cream and rust roses on a brown background, some trimmed with Nottingham lace on collars and cuffs, were marked down from £35 (already a low factory-shop price) to £16.50. Matching skirts were marked down from £35.50 to £20. Viyella cowl-neck blouses with dolman sleeves in a large teal-blue, avocado, turquoise, and violet paisley print were reduced from £45 to £16, and the matching skirts, from £55 to £25. Viyella shirts and blouses were marked down from £49 (a retail price ticket) to £12 for solids and £15 for prints and plaids, including a charming fox-hunting print on a sage green or red background.

Bright green cotton madras skirts were a summer bargain, marked down from £29.50 to £9.95, and a big-shouldered shawl-collared rust lamb's wool sweater was a great buy at £16, reduced from £49.

In accessories, best bets were leather belts. Wide red, brown, black, and navy waist wraps were reduced from £22 to only £4.50, and caramel or rust woven leather belts, from £20 to £3.50. Lace pantyhose in a 65-percent lamb's wool and 35-percent nylon blend were a wonderful buy at 75p. Incidentally, they came in very handy the next day, when the July weather in the north of England was 60°F and rainy.

For men, Van Heusen taupe or navy pure wool or wool-blend pants for £17.25 were a good buy, as were the Van Heusen wool-blend suits for £60 and £65. Allen Solly's sample cotton knit shirts cost only £8.

Little girls' dresses were quite pretty. White or pink polyester/cotton dresses with white and pink smocking were priced at £6. White cotton/polyester dresses with floral appliqués were £7.20, and sprigged floral cotton/polyester dresses with a white background were £7.50.

LONG EATON

CoxMoore of England
Broad Street
Long Eaton
Tel. (0602) 730361

Tues.–Sat. 10:00–4:00
Cash only (possibly credit cards by 1987)

Theoretically, CoxMoore makes only men's knit-wear. Actually, though, many of the sweaters and socks are quite attractive on women, so most women simply ignore the labels. CoxMoore supplies Harrods and Austin Reed in London, as well as many smaller boutiques, but here at the factory shop, prices are much lower—often below wholesale.

Pure cashmere socks near the cash register are the first great buy you generally see. At £4 for midcalf and £5 for over-the-calf lengths, they should be snapped up. (They usually cost over $50 in New York.) There is usually a good choice of colors: navy, medium blue, wine, and gray.

In sweaters, look for labels that read "PD," which stands for "Perfect Discontinued." These are often the best buys. A man's white cotton sweater with yellow shoulder patches and red and blue stripes bearing this tag and a Harrods label was £17.50. Another Harrods cotton sweater, in primrose cotton with narrow beige and white stripes—also a perfect discontinued—was only £15. Also on the sale rack were a khaki lamb's wool V-neck with multicolor stripes on the sleeves for £10, a fuchsia lamb's wool crewneck for £13.50, and an orange lamb's wool cable and puff-stitch crewneck—a sample sweater—for only £5.

CoxMoore does a nice collection of cashmere sweaters. V-neck cardigans with two pockets are £42.50 and £47.50 in such discontinued but classic colors as beige, medium blue, olive, pink, red, primrose, and navy. Very fine botany wool turtlenecks in red, white, beige, gray, and yellow are £12.50 and £14.50.

Men's Swiss cotton short-sleeved shirts in light khaki, peach, yellow, pale green, light blue, and medium blue cost only £9.50.

Unbelievable bargains lie in wait in the button box, where all buttons, including leather and metal ones, cost only 1p each. They make marvelous earrings, too. You see, you can still buy something nice for a penny!

MATLOCK

John Smedley Limited
Lea Mills
Matlock
Derbyshire DE4 5AG
Tel. (062984) 571

Mon.–Fri. 11:00–3:30, Sat.
10:00–3:00
Traveler's checks in pounds

It's hard to write about a factory outlet that may have as many as 3,500 sweaters and knitted shirts for sale at any one time.

One of the high points of Smedley's collection is its Verlana extra-fine Australian merino wool sweaters for men and women. With fibers as fine as those of cashmere, this luxury yarn, exclusive to Smedley, knits up into sweaters that are very expensive in London and the United States but very inexpensive at the factory shop. Most styles for men and women, in a range of 22 colors, are only £20 to £25. Intarsia (patterned) sweaters may be slightly higher.

Sea Island cotton is the cashmere of summer. At Smedley, V-neck and turtleneck sweaters and long- and short-sleeved shirts in this cool, luxurious fabric are available in up to 20 solid colors. (The men's shirts are elegant enough to be worn with a suit and tie.) For casual wear, the shirts also come in over a dozen striped color combinations. Their price: an unbelievable £15–£20.

Last, but surely not to be slighted at £10–£15, are Smedley's classic sweaters for men and women in light- and medium-weight botany wool, which come in over 30 colors.

Smedley's is certainly a place to visit to buy sweaters and knit shirts in one of every color: for yourself, for your family, and for your friends as gifts.

Pleasley Vale

William Hollins "Viyella"
Viyella Mills
Pleasley Vale
Tel. (0623) 810345

Mon., Wed.–Fri. 9:30–1:00
and 2:00–4:30, Sat.
9:30–12:30; closed Tues.
Cash only

See p. 70 for a complete write-up of this chain of factory shops specializing in Viyella, a luxury blend of 55 percent wool and 45 percent cotton.

Somercotes

William Hollins "Viyella"
Viyella House
Nottingham Road
Somercotes
Tel. (0773) 602201

Tues.–Fri. 10:00–12:00 and
12:30–4:00, Sat.
9:00–12:00
Cash only

This shop is one of three William Hollins "Viyella" factory outlets in the Nottingham area, all with slightly different hours. Only the Pleasley Vale shop (see above) is open on Monday, but it is the only one closed on Tuesday.

See p. 70, the Hucknall branch, for a complete write-up of this chain of factory shops specializing in Viyella, a luxury blend of 55 percent wool and 45 percent cotton.

SUTTON-IN-ASHFIELD

Elbeo Ltd
50 Stoney Street
Sutton-in-Ashfield
Nottinghamshire NG17 4GZ
Tel. (0623) 555000

Tues., Thurs., Fri.
11:30–3:00
Cash only

Elbeo is one of Britain's leading manufacturers of tights and stockings—no longer inexpensive, pedestrian items, but high-fashion, upmarket accessories that can cost over $25 in the United States.

Elbeo's own label and its Martyn Fisher Collection tights, pantyhose, and stockings are sold in the best department stores in London and in specialty shops in the United States and abroad.

The factory shop—unfortunately open only 10½ hours a week—is crammed with Elbeo's full range of products, including many end-of-season designs at large discounts. It certainly pays to think ahead to next fall and winter when 65 percent wool/35 percent nylon lace pantyhose in such glorious colors as black, burgundy, fudge, navy, nutmeg, plum, slate, snow, beaver, crocus, ivory, and tempest (blue-gray tweed) are selling at only £2 per pair, compared to London prices of £8.95 earlier in the year. Plain ribbed pantyhose in 50 percent wool/50 percent nylon in the same colors were £1.99

per pair, compared to London prices of £5.50. Stock changes rapidly, but discounts are at least 60 percent and sometimes as high as 80 percent. Elbeo's wonderful leg fashions should be bought by the dozen, especially by women who live in cold climates and love hard-to-find warm wool high-fashion tights.

Chapter 7 *Bradford*

Bradford isn't easy to reach by train, especially from Nottingham, which is only about 50 miles away, but it's worth the trip if you are looking for some of the best buys in luxury yarns, fabrics, and knitwear. (It will be faster and easier to rent a car or take a bus.) This ancient town, a center for the wool market for over 500 years, offers the greatest bargains I've seen in cashmere sweaters and accessories, wool knitwear, fine alpaca, wool and silk yarns, and superb fabrics.

Unlike Stoke-on-Trent, most factory outlets do not accept credit cards, so make sure that you bring enough cash or traveler's checks. You won't want to miss out on cashmere sweaters for as little as £16 just because you've run short of cash.

BRADFORD CITY

British Mohair Spinners
Midland Mills
Valley Road
Bradford BD1 4RL
Tel. (0274) 728456

Mon.–Fri. 11:00–3:00
VISA/Barclaycard,
MasterCard/Access,
traveler's checks in pounds

See p. 91 for a complete write-up of the main outlet, located in Keighley (it offers shoppers much longer hours).

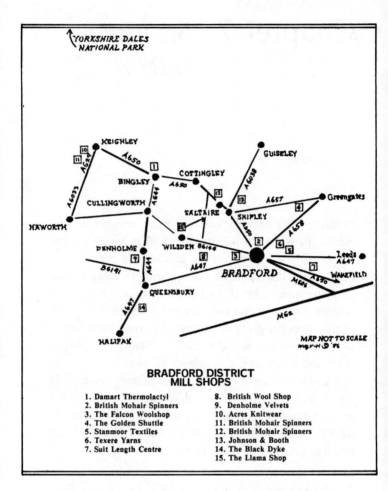

BRADFORD DISTRICT
MILL SHOPS

1. Damart Thermolactyl
2. British Mohair Spinners
3. The Falcon Woolshop
4. The Golden Shuttle
5. Stanmoor Textiles
6. Texere Yarns
7. Suit Length Centre
8. British Wool Shop
9. Denholme Velvets
10. Acres Knitwear
11. British Mohair Spinners
12. British Mohair Spinners
13. Johnson & Booth
14. The Black Dyke
15. The Llama Shop

Bradford's factory shops are clustered within a
20-mile radius and offer shoppers wonderful
bargains in fabrics, yarns, and clothing.

The British Wool Shop
Oak Mills
Station Road
Clayton
Bradford BD14 6JD
Tel. (0274) 880612

Mon.–Fri. 9:00–5:30, Sat. 10:00–4:00
VISA/Barclaycard, MasterCard/Access, traveler's checks in pounds
Mail order

The British Wool Shop is run by the British Wool Marketing Board, an industry group created to promote the use of wool and to educate the public about the yarns and cloth produced by the different breeds of sheep raised in Britain.

Display cases of sweaters that have been discontinued from the shop's catalog offer some of the best buys. Men's and women's camel or blue crewnecks were £6.99, and beautiful olive or rust moss-stitch boatneck sweaters were only £6.95, one of the best prices I've seen for pure wool sweaters. Checkerboard-pattern sweaters in sage/rust/cream were £14.75; the same sweaters in gray/blue/navy were fully priced at £19.25. Other sweaters in the group ranged from £5.95 to £18.

Designer sweater kits for hand knitters, including all yarns and all trimming, sold for £11.50 and £13.50, and pure wool skirt lengths in a variety of tweeds, for £5. However, hats, priced here at £11.85 and £12.75, were a better buy at the Black Dyke Mill Shop in Queensbury (see p. 93), where they were only £8.95. Men's wool socks in gray, navy, cinnamon, and sage green were £2.65, £2.85, and £5.45, depending on the length.

Men's Harris tweed jackets were also a good buy at £54.95 and £59.95, as was a woman's suit in a subtle bird's-eye tweed of brown and gray for £67.95.

Car rugs measuring 56 by 72 inches in tartans of Dress Gordon, Royal Stuart, Buchanan, and Dress Stuart are priced at £19.50. Smaller "knee" rugs, measuring 40 by 56 inches, in the more muted tartans of Mackenzie, MacDonald, and Hunting MacLeod are £11.50. Beautiful travel rugs measuring 54 by 72 inches in natural Jacob wool cost £19.75 for check or twill patterns. (The Jacob sheep is a rare four-horned breed that gets its name because of its multicolor coat: cream, beige, and dark brown patches.) Natural Jacob wool shawls measuring 45 by 45 inches in light or dark checks are £12.75, and 28-by 28-inch headsquares and 10-by 50-inch scarves in a variety of solids and checks are priced at £3.50.

Prime-quality sheepskins sell for £19.95, and unusual sheepskin polishing mitts, for £3.68. Sheepskin innersoles are only £1.95. Felt-trimmed sheepskin toys make excellent baby presents. The teddy bear is £11.75, the sheep £11.25, the lamb £7.75, the seal £9.75, the floppy-eared dog £9.50, the baby owl £4.75, and the mouse only £1.95. The Jacob sheep is £4.20, while the small sheep is £3.75.

For lovers of horse brasses, six breeds of sheep are depicted: Suffolk, Blackface, Wensleydale, Cheviot, Swaledale, and Jacob. The brasses alone cost £1.55; with black leather backing, they are £3.

Falcon Woolshop
118 Sunbridge Road
Bradford BD1 2NE
Tel. (0274) 722 385

Mail order:
Falcon-by-Post
Falcon Mills
Bartle Lane
Bradford BD7 4QJ
Tel. (0274) 576702 (for
  credit-card oreders)

Mon.–Sat. 9:00–5:00
VISA/Barclaycard,
  MasterCard/Access,
  traveler's checks in pounds
Mail order

Falcon Woolshop's sister company, Falcon-by-Post, is one of the largest mail-order suppliers of knitting yarns in the United Kingdom. It is an excellent source of inexpensive natural and synthetic yarns in both balls and the slightly more economical 200- to 500-gram cones (approximately 7 to 16½ ounces) for the serious knitter.

One of the pleasant features of *Falcon's Book of Wools,* a $2 catalog by mail (50p at the Bradford shop), is a list of the yarn's specifications next to the color samples. For example, Superwash, a machine-washable pure wool yarn, is available as double knitting yarn (a worsted weight) whose length is approximately 124 meters per 50-gram ball, with a gauge of 22 stitches to 10 cm (4 inches) on 4-mm (U.S. No. 5) needles, and costs 92p per ball. Superwash 4-ply, a slightly thinner yarn, has a length of approximately 200 meters per 50-gram ball, with a gauge of 28 stitches to 10 cm on 3¼-mm (U.S. No. 3) needles, and costs 94p per ball. The yarn comes in 22 glorious colors, including the luscious wild rose, begonia, mulberry, soft green, apricot, and French cream.

Shetland is a machine-washable wool yarn that comes in 12 shades, many of them lovely, subtle tweeds with names evocative of the islands: Rhum, Hebrides, Benbecula, Stronsay. Knitters will get 24 stitches to 10 cm on 3¾-mm (U.S. No. 4) needles. The yarn costs £1.05 for a 50-gram ball.

For knitters who like to work on larger needles, Lopi-Lyng is a lightweight hand-washable Icelandic bulky wool yarn that comes in heather (brown), clover (purplish rust), and cream (white). It works up on 6½-mm (U.S. No. 10) needles, with a gauge of 14 stitches to 10 cm, and costs 99p for a 50-gram ball.

At present Falcon-by-Post offers three cotton yarns in the same price range as the wools; Falcon Woolshop offers many more. There are also many synthetic yarns and blends, for those who prefer knitting with acrylic or nylon.

Falcon Woolshop and Falcon-by-Post offer a small variety of buttons, as well as knitting needles, crochet hooks, stitch holders, and row counters.

Stanmoor Textiles Ltd.

Providence Mills
Harris Street
Leeds Road
Bradford BD1 5JA
Tel. (0274) 727491

Thurs.–Fri. 10:00–5:00, Sat. 10:00–4:00
Traveler's checks in pounds

There are two things I like especially about this shop: its extraordinarily low prices and its honest labeling system, in which perfect merchandise bears the maker's original cloth label and slight seconds carry a small stick-on label.

Women's cashmere sweaters were on sale at the lowest prices I've seen in many years. Single-ply wine-colored V-neck sweaters were reduced 20 percent from their original low price of £19.50, for a sale price of only £15.60. Two-ply Scottish cashmere V-neck sweaters in a variety of colors were marked down from £29.99 to £22.50. Short-sleeved cashmere sweaters in yellow, beige, and black, originally £18.50–£25 were reduced 20 percent, to £14.80–£20.

Fine wool sweaters in solids and stripes, a bargain at their original prices of £6.99–£10.50, were marked down 20 percent, to £5.59–£8.40. Bowed sweaters in gray or wine were especially pretty at their low price of £5.59. Women's lamb's wool V-neck sweaters in light blue, royal blue, yellow, camel, and turquoise and ca-bled crewnecks in the same colors were reduced 20 percent—from £8.99 to £7.19. A special group of Fair Isle wool vests was only £3.50.

Women's soft gathered gray or rust Viyella (55 percent wool and 45 percent cotton) skirts were on sale for only £6.99—a wonderful buy, as the fabric alone cost £15.

For men, the best bets were perfect wool sweaters in solids and argyle patterns, in crewnecks, turtlenecks, and side-buttoned necks, for only £12.50 and £12.99.

Note: Stanmoor may have moved by publication date. If you cannot find the shop in the telephone directory, please check with the Bradford Economic Development Unit (0274) 753787.

Suit Length Centre

Bateman Ogden & Co. Ltd.
Argyll House
918 Wakefield Road
Bradford BD4 7QQ
Tel. (0274) 729103

Mon.–Sat. 8:30–5:00
VISA/Barclaycard,
*   MasterCard/Access,*
*   traveler's checks in pounds*
Mail order

This shop has the best selection of luxury suiting and coating fabrics in Bradford, starting with a 75-percent cashmere 25-percent wool coating fabric for only £14.50 per yard. The 60-inch-wide fabric comes in six classic colors: light and dark camel, light and dark gray, navy, and black.

Most fabrics are priced as 3½-yard suit lengths, but are also available by the yard. A sophisticated gray/white/wine plaid in lightweight wool, for a man's or woman's suit, was £31.90 for a suit length and £9.11 per yard. A 12 percent cashmere/88 percent wool fabric in navy/white or gray/white pinstripes or chalk stripes or in solid fawn or gray was £42 for a suit length and £12 per yard. The finest fabrics run from around £30 to £50 per suit length.

Remnants at the front of the shop offer excellent values. A cashmere/mink/wool navy or gray pinstripe was a standout at £9.90 for a one-yard piece—enough for a skirt or a vest. Other women's skirt lengths in wool tweeds or plaids range from around £4.50 to £10.50 and are located upstairs.

The shop also sells sweaters and shirts for men and women at substantial discounts. Men's wool crewnecks in beige, camel, olive, brown, gray, and blue were £13.50, and argyle vests in the same colors, £9.90. Men's Peter Scott Fair Isle sweaters with a patterned chest and navy sleeves and back cost £14.90. A small diamond-patterned crewneck in blue/gray/navy, blue/navy/wine, or gray/wine/red was £16.90. The shop also has the best prices for motif sweaters in shades of brown and beige; they looked like Jacob wool but were unlabeled. The strawberry, cherry, and Icelandic patterns were all only £19.90.

At £45, men's cashmere sweaters were a good buy, with both solids of gray, rose, or olive and a wine/tan/white pattern. Men's solid and striped cotton shirts were a better buy at Acres Knitwear (see p. 90), which had John Smedley solid and striped cotton shirts for £8.95. Here a lesser label was priced at £10.90 and £11.90.

Harris tweed caps were £5.50. Men's shearling gloves were £12.90, and women's, £12.20.

Wool and sheepskin rugs were also good buys. Wool travel rugs in plaids and stripes cost £12.50 and £16.50, depending on the size. A large, dramatic brown and beige Jacob wool travel rug was £19.80. Fluffy white single sheepskins were £19.50, and doubles, £35.

Texere Yarns
College Mill
Barkerend Road
Bradford BD3 9AQ
Tel. (0274) 722191

Mon.–Thurs. 9:00–12:00
and 1:30–4:30, Fri.
9:00–12:00 and
1:30–4:00, Sat. morning
by appointment only
Traveler's checks in pounds
Mail order

This three-story yarn warehouse, a short uphill climb from Bradford's British Rail station, is a joy to hand knitters and crocheters unable to find beautiful natural-fiber yarns at less than stratospheric prices. I can't praise enough the quality and variety of the yarns or the helpfulness of the staff.

Pure wool yarn comes in many weights and textures. Pure shetland yarn in over a dozen heathery colors is 55p per 25-gram ball. A sport-yarn weight in solids and some tweeds is £3 per 250-gram cone. A worsted weight (called double knitting yarn) is 45p per 50-gram ball; tweed yarns of about the same weight are 35p per 50-gram ball and £3 per 1-pound cone. Bulky (called chunky) is £1 per 100-gram ball, and Icelandic texture, 90p per 100-gram ball.

Cotton yarns are just as varied. A cotton slub (crinkle-textured) yarn in Jordan almond colors is £6.50 per 450-gram cone—enough for an adult sweater. A thinner cotton slub bouclé yarn in these and darker colors, including black and navy, is £6.50 per 1-pound cone. A silky 2-ply cotton is £3.30 per 250-gram cone.

Silk yarns are abundant, too. A 3-fold silk noil (rough-textured) yarn in bright colors and black is £7 per 350-gram cone; a thicker, shiny silk is £6.50 per 100-gram hank; and a Swiss-made blend of 50 percent silk and 50 percent wool is £1 per 20-gram ball.

Pure alpaca in muted colors such as pale blue, pale coral, faded denim, raspberry, and ashes-of-roses pink, is £1.70 per 50-gram ball—a much better buy than the 25-gram balls for £1.89 in grays and browns I saw the previous day in a Manchester department store. I think this alpaca has a better feel to it than the more expensive blend of 85 percent cashmere and 15 percent wool, whose colors are more limited.

In addition to all of these stock items, Texere also has many end-of-lot specials. Pure alpaca yarn was only £4 per 1-pound cone—a great buy if you like fawn or gray. Many one- or few-of-a-kind balls of yarn are bunched into "craft packs" at £2 per ½-kilogram (1.1-pound) pack.

Note: Texere has a very large and well-organized mail-order department. Address mail-order questions to Mr. Keith Nichols, Inquiries.

BINGLEY

Damart Thermolactyl

Bowling Green Mills, off
  Park Road
Bingley
West Yorkshire BD16 4BH
Tel. (0274) 568234

Mon.–Sat. 9:00–5:00
VISA/Barclaycard,
  MasterCard/Access,
  traveler's checks in pounds
Mail order

Damart barely squeaks into this book—it's not really a factory shop but a catalog store. With rare exceptions, the merchandise is the same price here as it is in the mail-order catalog. I include Damart only because retail prices here are still much lower than in the United States, where skiers and winter-sports lovers swear by the company's variety of warm and stylish winter underwear.

Women's underwear comes in sizes 8–28 (dress sizes) in white, cream, champagne, honey, oatmeal, pink, light blue, burgundy, bright red, and black. Colors and large sizes usually cost more than whites and smaller sizes. Among the prettiest winter underwear: lace-trimmed camisoles and vests for £3.75–£6.50, twin-packs of briefs for £5.25–£8.25, and single pairs of tap pants (called French knickers) for £5.99 in white and £6.25 in pink for sizes 10–20, and £6.65 in white and £7.25 in pink for size 22/24.

For colder weather, the long-sleeved top (called a spencer) and matching long pants are a good idea. The tops are £6.75 in white and £7.45 in black, scarlet, or burgundy for sizes 10–16; in the larger sizes, they are £8.25 in white and £8.99 in colors. Double Force Thermolactyl underwear, billed as "The Warmest Ladies' Underwear in the World," for maximum protection from freezing weather, comes in white, light blue, and navy. The long-sleeved top costs £14.75 in white and £15.75 in colors for sizes 10–20; they are £16.75 in white and £18.75 in colors for size 22/24. Long pants cost £13.25 in white and £14.75 in colors for sizes 10–20, and £14.25 in white and £15.75 in colors for size 22/24.

A luxury blend of 15 percent silk and 85 percent Thermolactyl made its appearance in the fall of 1986 in four beautiful lace-trimmed ivory pieces: a nightgown for £27.50, a short-sleeved vest for £11.99, a camisole, also for £11.99, and tap pants for £6.25. All come in sizes 10–24, with no extra charge for the larger sizes.

For men, T-shirts (called short-sleeved vests) come in white, navy, light blue, burgundy, and oatmeal. The T-shirts cost £7.75 in white and £8.50 in colors for sizes 33–44 inches, and £8.75 in white and £9.99 in colors for sizes 45–52 inches. Matching long pants cost £8.99 in white and £10.50 in colors and in white extra-long for sizes 29–40 inches; for sizes 41–48 inches, they are £10.85 in white and £11.99 in colors and in white extralong.

Damart's Double Force Thermolactyl underwear is available as a long-sleeved top and pants in white, navy, and denim blue. The shirts cost £16.50 in white and £18.50 in colors for sizes 33–44 inches, and £18.99 in white and £21.50 in colors for size 45/48 inches. Matching pants are priced at £14.99 in white and £16.99 in colors for sizes 29–40 inches, and £16.99 in white and £18.99 in colors for size 41/44 inches.

Knitted acrylic/Thermolactyl caps for men and women come in navy/red or navy/sky blue for £3.99.

Denholme

Denholme Velvets
Route A644
Denholme
Bradford BD13 4EZ
Tel. (0274) 832185

Mon.–Fri. 1:00–5:00, Sat.
9:00–5:00
Cash only

Note: Some fabrics are sold by the yard here, some by the meter.

Denholme Velvets manufactures and sells only velvet—as fabrics and as ladies' jackets and skirts. Cotton velvet skirts in wine, blue, red, gray, and black were marked down from an already low price of £11.95 to £7.95, and matching jackets were priced at a low £22.95.

Remnants in 48-inch-wide rayon velvet were £2.55 per meter in a rich wine, teal blue, brown, and black. The same velvet on the bolt, in turquoise, spice, violet, and red, was £4.95 per meter, and in navy and black, £5.05 per meter. Embossed (self-color-patterned) velvets were more expensive, but clearly worth the price. Wine velvet with small flowers was £7.25 per meter; a red velvet with larger flowers was £6.35 per meter, as was my favorite, a dark green velvet with an embossed paisley pattern.

Cotton dress velvets in rust, ocher, red, gray, or green were £5.25 per yard. A black velvet with vertical stripes of silver Lurex at that price was a special buy. A medium blue and a spice-brown cotton velvet were on sale for only £3.25 per yard.

Washable cotton curtain velvets in 60-inch widths come in a rainbow of 25 colors for £6.95 per yard.

Handy people should check the remnant basket, where small pieces for making toys or covering coat hangers are priced at only 20p–30p.

GREENGATES

Golden Shuttle (Parkland)

Albion Mills
Albion Road
Greengates
Bradford BD10 9TQ
Tel. (0274) 611161
  Tues.–Fri.
(0274) 618035 Sat.

Tues.–Sat. 9:30–4:30
American Express,
  VISA/Barclaycard,
  MasterCard/Access,
  traveler's checks in pounds

Golden Shuttle is virtually a clothing department store. It stocks women's clothes in British sizes 10–24, men's in British sizes 36–48, and children's in sizes 0–12 years. Parkland, the parent company, manufactures the fabric, then buys up the ready-made garments from the companies that use it.

Women's cashmere coats are among the best buys. Classically styled single- or double-breasted designs with raglan or set-in sleeves, belted or unbelted, come in cream, fawn, camel, red, navy, chocolate, grape, and gray, and cost only £56.95 to £89.95, including VAT, compared with over £250 in London and over $500 in the United States. Most women's wool coats are priced under £60. Women's raincoats come in dozens of classic and trendy styles—all lined, some quilted—for £19.95–£37.95.

One of the most unusual women's items is a reversible wool skirt made of Parkland's fabric, manufactured by the Slimma, Gor-ray, and Two-Way Collection companies. These very attractive plaid pleated skirts are ideal for women who travel because each side of the reversible skirt has a different, but complementary, color palette. You get two skirts in one. Retail prices for these marvelous skirts are £70–£100; at

Golden Shuttle, they are only £36.95 for perfect-quality garments.

Women's classic wool suits by such British makers as Dalkeith, Reldan, Julius, and Ann Blair are only £30–£68—about half the retail price. To pop under them: Burberry V-neck lamb's wool sweaters for only £6.95. They come in only one color—cream—but £6.95 is still a bargain compared to £30–£40 for the same sweater in department stores. Women's pure wool tartan kilt skirts, complete with pin, are only £9.50.

Men's suits are available in wool or mohair, either single- or double-breasted, in navy, gray, beige, fawn, cream, and tweeds for £20–£64.95. Fly-fronted raincoats come in stone, navy, and olive green for under £30. Knitwear, shirts, ties, and belts by major British manufacturers are also available.

Best children's buys are little girls' dresses in checked or striped cotton with a pinafore in white broderie anglaise embroidery for £7.50 and pure wool kilts in sizes 1–12 for £5.99.

Home sewers are not forgotten. Pure wool worsteds and wool mixtures sell at the same price: 1 meter of 60-inch-wide fabric is £2, 1½ meters is £3, and a 3½-meter suit length of luxury fabric is £12.

KEIGHLEY

Acres Knitwear
Acres Mill
Berry Lane, off South Street
King Street
Keighley BD21 1DJ

Small sign on door:
T. Haley & Sons Ltd.
Reg. Office
Tel. (0535) 661429

Tues.–Fri. 10:30–5:00
Traveler's checks in pounds
Mail order

This mill shop sells its own knitwear, as well as scarves and knitwear made by such top manufacturers as Pringle, Lyle & Scott, and John Smedley.

The previous season's Pringle women's cashmere crewneck and turtleneck sweaters in such dark neutrals as brown, hunter green, navy, and black were only £38, with seconds selling for only £20. These seconds were slightly overmilled (washed and steamed a little too long), which gave them the feel that cashmeres get after their first washing or dry cleaning.

Women's Lyle & Scott lamb's wool sweaters at £31.50 and £36.95 were not as good a bargain, but came in a much greater variety of colors: khaki, mint, spruce, mink, rust, gray, cream, red, and aqua.

For men, John Smedley (see p. 73 for main listing) fine botany wool sweaters were good buys. Shirts were £13.25, turtlenecks £12.50, cardigans £13.50, crewnecks £12.50, V-neck sweaters £14, mock turtlenecks £10.50, and vests £10.50 and £11.50. John Smedley luxury Sea Island cotton shirts were priced lower here than anywhere in Bradford: £8.95 for solid colors or stripes.

My favorites were the pure cashmere stoles, with the 17-by 74-inch size selling for only £15.50 and the 29-by 74-inch size for £22.50. The colors were glorious: yellow, gray, black, green, turquoise, charcoal, old rose, tobacco, royal blue, camel, and white.

British Mohair Spinners
Grove Mills
Ingrow
Keighley BD21 5EG
Tel. (0535) 602293

Mon.–Sat. 9:00–4:00
VISA/Barclaycard,
MasterCard/Access,
traveler's checks in pounds

British Mohair Spinners is a hand-knitter's paradise, especially since the company's three shops—in

Keighley, Shipley, and Bradford—accept credit cards. (Most shops in the area don't.) Most of British Mohair's superb bargains are one-shots, but that shouldn't bother tourists, who know that they aren't likely to return soon. Just buy enough yarn so that you know you'll have enough to finish your knitting or crocheting project.

Rejected or canceled commercial orders are the best buys. Black or gray mohair, shot through with multicolor metallic strands, was priced at an incredible 1p per gram. The yarn had failed final inspection tests because it had been spun a little too thin to meet the design requirements of the customer, a sweater manufacturer. From a hand knitter's point of view, there was absolutely nothing wrong with the yarn. Plain kid mohair yarn in spruce green, rust, violet, cream, and ocher was only a little less of a bargain at £1.36 per 50 grams.

Pure Welsh wool in olive or wine, with multicolor strands, was only £1 per 400- to 500-gram hank. Imagine being able to knit a wool suit for only £5—which is what I'll do when I finish writing this book. There are "oddment" boxes, which offer a variety of yarns for only £1 per hank—usually enough for a child's sweater. For an adult's sweater, you'll need two or three. The women at the shop are very knowledgeable and will gladly help you calculate your yarn requirements. (*Note:* Remember that British needle sizes are the reverse of U.S. sizes, and that the numbers add up to 13: the British 12 is a U.S. 1, and the British 2 is a U.S. 11.)

British Mohair Spinners also carries merchandise from other manufacturers, usually end-of-season items at bargain prices. John Smedley V-neck and crewneck fine wool sweaters for men and women in taupe, gold, light blue, turquoise, ocher, and rose were marked down to £6.99. The same sweaters in the more classic colors of brown, navy, wine, gray, and hunter green were £12.99. (See p. 73 for a complete write-up of John Smedley.)

Pure wool travel rugs were a good buy at £20, as were mohair travel rugs at £32. A rack of sweaters offered some £10 bargains, including machine-knit Aran-style sweaters in cream wool, and very heavy double-knit ribbed crewnecks in cream, navy, or brown wool.

Cashmere sweaters—turtlenecks, V-necks, and crewnecks that zipped up the back—made in England and in China were sale-priced at £29. The sweaters in red, blue, gray, and other fashion colors that were made in England were a better buy than the fawn and brown sweaters made in China. Both were superior to Hong Kong cashmeres, which usually sell for $75–$100 in the United States.

QUEENSBURY

Black Dyke Mill Shop

John Foster and Son
Main Street
Queensbury
Bradford BD13 1QA
Tel. (0274) 880285

Mon.–Sat. 10:00–1:00,
1:45–4:30
Traveler's checks in pounds

The Black Dyke Mill is directly behind the shop and exports most of its woven fabric to Japan, where it is made into high-quality men's suits. Ends of bolts wind up here, where men's suiting in fine mohair/wool blends costs only £6 per meter. Wool skirt lengths cost as little as £2, and trouser lengths, as little as £5. There are even a few below-mill-cost pieces at £1 per meter.

Solid, printed, or plaid men's shirts of Viyella, that

luxury fabric blend of 55 percent wool and 45 percent cotton, are only £12.95 here—slightly cheaper than in Viyella's own William Hollins shops in the Nottingham area (see p. 70). Men's extra-fine merino sweaters (called botany) are £6.95–£10.95 in V-necks, turtlenecks, or crewnecks in a wide variety of colors, with shades of blue, coral, and beige predominating.

Men's suits are £50–£75, including a handsome navy pinstripe wool for £55, and jackets are £40–£60, including a classic brown and beige herringbone wool for £45. All hats are £8.95—the best price I found in Bradford—and the English country hat and deerstalker in wool plaids and tweeds of gray, brown, rust, and green would be equally attractive on women as on men. Caps in the same wool fabrics are £6.95—also the best price in the vicinity.

Most women's sweaters are £12.95, with fine lamb's wool and merino sweaters selling for £16.95. This group includes intarsia sweaters, in which a colored pattern is knitted into the sweater. Among the prettiest in the group: a cream cowl-neck sweater, with zigzag stripes of brown, rust, and mint green.

SHIPLEY

British Mohair Spinners
Lower Holme Mills
Baildon
Shipley BD17 7EU
Tel. (0274) 583111

Mon.–Sat. 9:00–4:00
VISA/Barclaycard,
MasterCard/Access,
traveler's checks in pounds

See p. 91 for a complete write-up of the main outlet, located in Keighley. Both this shop and the one in Keighley have much better shopping hours than the outlet in Bradford, which is open only until 3:00 and which is closed on Saturday.

The Llama Shop
Salts Mill
Victoria Road
Saltaire
Shipley BD18 3LB
Tel. (0274) 581121

Mon.–Sat. 9:30–5:00; closed
Wed. 1:00–2:00
VISA/Barclaycard,
MasterCard/Access

The Llama Shop is located in Saltaire, a famous and fascinating Victorian model town built by the industrialist Sir Titus Salt for his factory workers. The shop carries fabric and knitwear manufactured by a group of affiliated companies at low prices.

Sale-rack women's wool sweaters—always a good place to start—ranged from £8.95 to £20. Especially attractive were a wine cowl for £19.50, a pale peach cabled and latticed sweater for £10.50, and a cheerful red cardigan, also for £10.50.

In fabrics, pure wool 60-inch-wide tweeds in beiges, grays, browns, and greens were a good buy at £5.95 per yard. Suit lengths were £17 and £17.50; a charcoal brown pinstripe was especially nice. The fabrics, while not as luxurious as those carried by the Suit Length Centre in Bradford (see p. 83), were also less than half their price.

Wool coat and skirt fabric in 60-inch widths started at £5 per yard and looked most attractive in solid flannels of gray, navy, olive, rose, rust, and black. A luxury coating blend of 60 percent wool and 40 percent camel was £7.45 per yard and came in white, green, black, blue, rust, and camel.

Wool/mohair travel rugs in a variety of plaids were £24, and larger throws, suitable for covering beds, were £31.50.

Scarves in a blend of 70 percent cashmere and 30 percent wool were a bargain at £8.95—they were £12.50 elsewhere—and came in light blue, dusty rose, violet, bright yellow, primrose, wine, and black. Shearling gloves were also a bargain here, compared to other places, at £10.95 for men's gloves, £9.50 for women's, and £2.75 for children's mittens. Shearling slippers were £8.85 and £10.25.

Checked and striped accessories made of Jacob wool—from the rare four-horned brown and white Jacob sheep—were a good buy here, with caps at £7.95, scarves at £3.50, and shawls at £12.50.

WILSDEN

Johnson & Booth
Mill Shop
Main Street
Wilsden
Bradford BD15 0BE
Tel. (0535) 272202

Mon.–Fri. 1:30–4:30, Sat.
in Nov.–Dec. 10:00–4:00
Cash only

Although this small shop has limited hours and does not accept credit cards, it offers excellent buys in sweaters and leather gloves for men and women.

Ladies' cashmere sweaters—many made by Lyle & Scott—were £25 and £30, prices lower than many I have seen in Scotland. Most sweaters are solid-color classics, but there are a few patterned sweaters that are especially good buys, such as a light blue cowl-neck sweater for £30 with nutmeg sleeves that have pencil-thin blue and white stripes. Black cashmere pleated skirts were wonderful buys at £35; they usually cost well over £100 in London and over $200 in New York. Among the one-of-a-kinds, a Lyle & Scott hooded beige cashmere sweatshirt with a leather tie was only £35.

Men's cashmere sweaters are bargains, too, at £37.50 and £37.90 for classic colors and styles and a few patterned designs.

Ladies' lamb's wool sweaters come in a variety of

styles. V-neck cardigans in sapphire and shocking pink were £13.50; lamb's wool shirts in yellow or beige, £11.75; and tie-necks in black or white, only £10.50. A navy cardigan with a vertically striped red, white, and blue ribbon trim down the center was an excellent buy at £9.50, as were a group of John Smedley mock turtleneck and V-neck merino sweaters, marked down to £10.25 in an end-of-season clearance.

Make sure to check the bargain boxes at the entrance. A recent visit turned up a man's cabled blue shetland sweater for only £9.50, a hunter green wool sweater with a wine/navy/white argyle pattern for £10, and a sleeveless cream wool cabled V-neck sweater with navy trim for £10.25. The £5 bargain box contained many one-of-a-kind sweaters, including a woman's gray merino turtleneck and a white wool V-neck cardigan with a blue argyle pattern.

Leather gloves are also excellent bargains. Men's lambskin gloves are £13.99, and women's, £11.99. Cape leather gloves for both men and women are £8.25 unlined, £10.25 lined with wool, and £11.95 lined with silk. Pigskin gloves are £9.75 for men and £7.99 for women. Driving gloves sell for £5.25. Golfing gloves cost £3.25 and £4.50, and women's crochet-backed leather gloves are priced at only £3.99.

Chapter 8 *The Rest of England*

ᏬᎲᏮᎲᏮᎲᏮ

This chapter might well be called "The Best of the Rest." Because these factory shops are scattered all over England, rather than being clustered in towns, as in the earlier chapters, think of these factory shops as places to visit if you are in the vicinity, rather than planning a trip around them. Fortunately, many of these shops have a mail-order service, so you can order from them without detouring to visit them.

BATH

Reject China
34–36 Stall Street
Bath
Tel. (0225) 62977

Mon.–Sat. 9:00–6:00, Sun.
10:00–6:00 Oct.–May;
Mon.–Sat. 9:00–7:00,
Sun. 10:00–7:00
June–Sept.
American Express, Diners
Club, VISA/Barclaycard,
MasterCard/Access,
traveler's checks in pounds
Mail order; mailing list;
visits to some U.S. cities in
fall

See p. 36 for a complete write-up of the main store, located in London.

BIRMINGHAM

Angora Silver Plate Co. Ltd.
3 Regent Street
Birmingham B1 3HG
Tel. (021) 236 5362

Mon.–Fri. 9:30–5:00
Cash only
Mail order

Angora Silver Plate is a major manufacturer of sterling, silverplate, and pewter giftware, and will sell to private visitors at wholesale prices.

There is a small collection in hallmarked sterling silver. Baby gifts are available at unbeatable prices. A rabbit or teddy bear rattle is £14.25, and a spoon, £14.90; baby cups range from £51.55 to £73.65. For adults, a set of six teaspoons in a simple elegant pattern costs £64.25 boxed and £69 in a dark blue leatherette and white satin case. Coffee spoons in the same pattern cost £33.55 boxed and £36.45 in a case. A 4½- by 3-inch oval picture frame is £29. Plain napkin rings—ideal for monogramming—are £11 for the ½-inch width and £14.80 for the 1-inch width. Wine labels are £6.05 each. Also available in hallmarked sterling silver are a butter knife for £5.95, a cake knife for £12.20, a cheese knife for £8.10, a letter opener for £9.65, and a pie server for £11.85.

True to its name, Angora really excels in silver-plate items, both in its extensive selection and in price. Where there was one sterling picture frame, there are a half dozen in silverplate, ranging from £5.45 for a 4¼- by 3¼-inch rectangle to £15.80 for an 8- by 10½-inch rectangle. Instead of three sterling silver baby cups, there are ten sold separately from £4.75 to £10.45, and another dozen or two sold as parts of sets. Top of the line is the 11-piece presentation set for £45, comprising a bowl, a cup, a brush, an egg stand, a baby spoon, a napkin ring, a child's knife, fork, and spoon, a loop-handled spoon, and a food pusher. Of course, many smaller sets are available in the £5–£15 range, and the rabbit, teddy bear, and three other rattle designs are only £2.65.

Many silverplate items are ideal for entertaining or as gifts. An 8-inch punch bowl is £34.30; the larger 12-inch bowl is £51.40. Either one fits on a footed scalloped 16-inch tray for £31.70, and individual-handled punch cups are £6.25 each. A one-pint cocktail shaker costs £20.75; a brandy warmer, £10.80; a half-pint Georgian-style mug, £13.15, and its larger one-pint brother, £14.25; and a straight-sided one-pint mug, £15.55.

A simple low two-light candelabrum costs only £8.70; others range from £7.05 to £44.25 for an 11¼-inch five-light candelabrum. Simple candlesticks are priced at £6.80 for the 4-inch size, and a candle snuffer costs £5.65.

For breakfast, a set comprising egg cup, stand, and spoon costs £7, and a silverplate toast rack with nylon feet is £10.40. For dinner, a footed 6½-inch-diameter rose bowl with a beaded wavy edge, lion-head handles, and a wire-mesh interior for flower arrangement could double as a wine cooler. Its price: only £14.60. For any time, a three-piece condiment set on a stand for £7.70 and a footed open sugar bowl with an embossed rim and matching spoon for £10.85 would cheer up any table.

CANTERBURY

Reject China
14 High Street
Canterbury
Tel. (0227) 470518

Mon.–Sat. 9:00–6:00, Sun. 10:00–6:00 Oct.–May; Mon.–Sat. 9:00–7:00, Sun. 10:00–7:00 June–Sept.
American Express, Diners Club, VISA/Barclaycard, MasterCard/Access, traveler's checks in pounds
Mail order; mailing list; visits to some U.S. cities in fall

This branch of Reject China opened in 1986. See p. 36 for a complete write-up of the main store, located in London.

CHANNEL ISLANDS

Le Tricoteur & Co. Ltd
Pitronnerie Road
St. Peter Port
Guernsey, Channel Islands
Tel. (0481) 26214

Mon.–Fri. 8:00–12:30, 1:30–5:00
American Express, Diners Club, VISA/Barclaycard, MasterCard/Access, traveler's checks in pounds
Mail order
Telephone orders with credit cards during above hours

If you love the outdoors, especially sailing, traditional Guernsey sweaters are a must. Guernsey's knitting industry dates back to the early 16th century, and Guernsey knitwear was worn by Elizabeth I and Mary, Queen of Scots, and is worn by the present royal family. Guernseys have become virtually a generic term to describe the warm, hard-wearing, water-repellent sweater whose design has not changed essentially since the early 19th century. One important design feature: the diamond-shaped underarm gusset that gives the arm increased freedom of movement without straining the sweater. Ordinary sweaters given hard wear will develop holes under the arms, where four seams meet. The gusset of a guernsey reinforces this area.

Traditional guernseys range from £8 for the 22-inch size (20-inch chest) to £29 for the 54-inch size (52-inch chest), with most adult sizes (34–46 inches) only £21. Sizes up to 48 inches are available in traditional navy, corvette blue, Biscay blue (bright blue), tartan red, steel gray, new natural (beige), tobacco (dark brown), Goodwood green (hunter green), Breton red (rust), olive, Tudor red (bright wine), or Aran white.

Sizes 50, 52, and 54 inches are available in navy only.

Guernsey jackets with zippers and pockets come in navy, new natural, Tudor red, corvette blue, and steel gray, and are £26 in 36- and 38-inch sizes and £27 in 40- to 46-inch sizes. Hats are £3.10; scarves are £5 for the small size and £9 for the large size.

Count on adding approximately £5 per sweater if you want airmail delivery.

Even if you knit, I don't think it's worth buying the 5-ply yarn at £1.68 for a 100-gram skein to knit your own guernsey. At about £15 for 9 skeins for a 40-inch sweater, you're saving only £6 by doing it yourself. Order the sweater and have it knit by experts, but you may wish to consider buying the yarn for other hand-knitting projects.

CHEPSTOW

Stuart & Sons Ltd.
Bridge Street
Chepstow
Gwent NP6 5EZ
Tel. (02912) 70135

Mon.–Sun. 9:00–8:00
May–Sept.; Mon.–Sun.
9:00–5:00 Oct.–Apr.
American Express, Diners
Club, VISA/Barclaycard,
MasterCard/Access,
traveler's checks in pounds
Mail order—inquiry first

Note the lovely summer shopping hours—perhaps because this Stuart Crystal factory shop is so near the Chepstow Racecourse, Chepstow Castle, the St. Pierre Golf Course, the Chepstow Museum, and Tintern Abbey of Wordsworth fame.

See p. 105 for a complete write-up of Stuart Crystal stemware and accessories at the main shop, located in Stourbridge, England, and p. 179 for a complete write-up of Stuart Strathearn's sand-engraved crystal and colored crystal at the shop in Crieff, Scotland.

CHESTER

Reject China
5–7 Eastgate Street
Chester
Tel. (0244) 311592

Mon.–Sat. 9:00–6:00, Sun.
*   10:00–6:00 Oct.–May;*
*   Mon.–Sat. 9:00–7:00,*
*   Sun. 10:00–7:00*
*   June–Sept.*
American Express, Diners
*   Club, VISA/Barclaycard,*
*   MasterCard/Access,*
*   traveler's checks in pounds*
Mail order; mailing list;
*   visits to some U.S. cities in*
*   fall*

See p. 36 for a complete write-up of the main shop, located in London.

EXETER

Stuart Lighting Ltd.
St. Olaves Close
Mary Arches Street
Exeter EX4 3TP
Tel. (0392) 216573

Mon.–Sat. 9:00–5:30
American Express, Diners
*   Club, VISA/Barclaycard,*
*   MasterCard/Access,*
*   traveler's checks in pounds*
Mail order—inquire first

As its name suggests, this Stuart Crystal outlet emphasizes crystal lamps. It also carries a representative selection of Stuart Crystal merchandise and may be more convenient for you than Stuart's Stourbridge or Chepstow factory shops if you are heading toward the beaches in England's southwest.

See p. 105 for a complete write-up of Stuart Crystal stemware and accessories at the main store, located in Stourbridge, England, and p. 179 for a complete write-up of Stuart Strathearn's sand-engraved crystal and colored crystal at the shop in Crieff, Scotland.

MACCLESFIELD

J. Sheldon & Co. Ltd
Paradise Mill
Park Lane
Macclesfield
Cheshire SK11 6TL
Tel. (0625) 23146

Second Fri. of every month,
1:00–4:00
Traveler's checks in pounds

The bad news is that this manufacturer of beautiful infants' and children's clothing opens its factory shop only three hours every month. The good news is that its prices are so low that it's worth the trip if you are in England that day.

Located in the same building as Macclesfield's Working Silk Museum—worth a visit before or after your shopping spree—Sheldon sells its samples and end-of-the-season stock garments at incredibly low prices. Girls' dresses and boys' rompers or suits with short pants in cotton and wool blends are often trimmed with bows and rosebuds or original embroidered and appliquéd designs. Young girls' party dresses start at £5, and velvet dresses, at only £10. Wool-blend dresses start at £7, and romper sets, at £6; these are usually embroidered. Boys' romper sets and short suits start at around £4.

In addition to its children's clothing, Sheldon carries a wide range of fabrics and trimmings on sale, sometimes as low as £1 per yard.

Oxford

Reject China
54 Cornmarket Street
Oxford
Tel. (0865) 724301

Mon.–Sat. 9:00–6:00, Sun.
*   10:00–6:00 Oct.–May;*
Mon.–Sat. 9:00–7:00,
*   Sun. 10:00–7:00*
*   June–Sept.*
American Express, Diners
*   Club, VISA/Barclaycard,*
*   MasterCard/Access,*
*   traveler's checks in pounds*
Mail order; mailing list;
*   visits to some U.S. cities in*
*   fall*

See p. 36 for a complete write-up of the main store, located in London.

Stourbridge

Stuart & Sons Ltd.
Redhouse Glassworks
Wordsley
Stourbridge
West Midlands DY8 4AA
Tel. (0384) 71161

Mon.–Sun. 9:00–5:00
American Express, Diners
*   Club, VISA/Barclaycard,*
*   MasterCard/Access,*
*   traveler's checks in pounds*
Mail order—inquire first

Stuart Crystal's main factory outlet is in Stourbridge, the center of the British crystal industry. Beautiful hand-cut crystal has been made at the Stuart Redhouse Glassworks for over 250 years, and the Stuart family has been involved for over 150 years.

Crystal stemware and accessories are emphasized here, although the factory shop also has a number of sand-engraved and colored-crystal pieces sent down from Stuart Strathearn Limited, its Scottish subsidiary in Crieff (see p. 179). Slight seconds sell for about one-third less than the retail price, and discontinued first-quality pieces sell for half price, including VAT, so your net price is half or less of British retail prices and much less than half of U.S. retail prices.

Ariel, a pattern with a spiral air twist in its stem, is unusual and beautiful. The goblet and the champagne flute are each £14, the liqueur glass is £10.20, the 10-ounce rummer (old-fashioned glass) is £8.85, and the large square decanter is £50.

Monaco, an elegant, simple pattern of vertical lines, is comparatively inexpensive. The goblet and 12-ounce brandy snifter are each £8.65, the champagne flute is £7.50, the liqueur glass is £5.30, the 10-ounce rummer is £6.85, and the large square decanter is £33.35.

For stocking stuffers or hostess presents, look at Monaco's variety of perfume bottles and atomizers, selling at £4.35–£8.65, or the violet vase for £5.30. Larger straight-sided "tube" vases are £6.50 and £8.35. Executives might enjoy Monaco's crystal tankards; the ½-pint size is £10, and the 1-pint size, £13.30.

Senator's classic laurel-leaf-band motif and fluted columnar body set it apart from most traditional patterns. The goblet is £11.85, the champagne flute and large wineglass are £10.20, the liqueur glass is £7.20, the 10-ounce rummer is £9.20, and the large, square decanter is £43.35.

The Senator collection contains many beautiful table accessories. Footed bowls are £63.35 for the 10-inch size, £40 for the 8-inch size, and £21.70 for the 6-inch size. A stately 12-inch footed compote (called comport) costs £63.35. Urn vases—lovely for flowers or as lamps—are £40 for the 10-inch size and £20 for the 8-inch size. Crystal tankards are £13.30 for the ½-pint size and £17.50 for the pint. The "croft and up," a deskside or bedside water carafe topped with a matching tumbler, is priced at £17.85.

STRATFORD-UPON-AVON

Reject China
27 Bridge Street
Stratford-upon-Avon
Tel. (0789) 298042

Mon.–Sat. 9:00–6:00, Sun.
10:00–6:00 Oct.–May;
Mon.–Sat. 9:00–7:00,
Sun. 10:00–7:00
June–Sept.
American Express, Diners
Club, VISA/Barclaycard,
MasterCard/Access,
traveler's checks in pounds
Mail order; mailing list;
visits to some U.S. cities in
fall

This branch of Reject China opened in 1986. See
p. 36 for a complete write-up of the main shop, located
in London.

WINDSOR

Reject China
One Castle Hill
Windsor
Tel. (095) 50870

Mon.–Sat. 9:00–6:00, Sun.
10:00–6:00 Oct.–May;
Mon.–Sat. 9:00–7:00,
Sun. 10:00–7:00
June–Sept.
American Express, Diners
Club, VISA/Barclaycard,
MasterCard/Access,
traveler's checks in pounds
Mail order; mailing list;
visits to some U.S. cities in
fall

See p. 36 for a complete write-up of the main shop,
located in London.

WORCESTER

Royal Worcester Spode Ltd

Severn Street
Worcester WR1 2NE
Tel. (0905) 23221

*Mon.–Sat. 9:00–5:00
Oct.–Apr.; Mon.–Sat.
9:00–5:00, Sun.
10:00–5:00 May–Sept.;
open bank holidays except
Dec. 25–26 and Easter
Monday
American Express, Diners
Club, VISA/Barclaycard,
MasterCard/Access,
traveler's checks in pounds
Mail order*

Royal Worcester's factory shop sells perfect merchandise at retail prices and slight seconds at prices at least 25 percent below retail. During sale periods (approximately two and a half weeks in July and four weeks beginning Dec. 27), at least an additional 25 percent is deducted from seconds prices and up to 50 percent on some patterns. There are many other sale promotions during the year.

Seasonal sale prices are especially good. A 25-piece dinner service in the popular gold-edged harvest fruit-and-vegetable pattern of Evesham costs £191.90, including VAT, if perfect and £144.60 as slight seconds, but during the July 1986 sale, for example, the price for the set as slight seconds dropped to only £99.95, including VAT. The Evesham gold-edged 1¼-quart round soufflé dish, costing £10.05 if perfect and £7.30 as a slight second, was reduced to £3.65 during the sale. A 25-piece dinner service in Silver Jubilee, a new bone china pattern costing £228.10 if perfect and £165.75 as a slight second, was marked down to £123.41 during the sale.

Microwave owners: Royal Worcester has made a

number of its patterns without their gold or silver edges especially for microwave use.

YORK

Reject China
18/20 Stonegate
York
Tel. (0904) 644436

Mon.–Sat. 9:00–6:00, Sun. 10:00–6:00 Oct.–May; Mon.–Sat. 9:00–7:00, Sun. 10:00–7:00 June–Sept.
American Express, Diners Club, VISA/Barclaycard, MasterCard/Access, traveler's checks in pounds
Mail order; mailing list; visits to some U.S. cities in fall

See p. 36 for a complete write-up of the main store, located in London.

Part Three

Scotland

{ornamental divider}

Chapter 9 *Scotland: The Basics*

Scotland is as bonny as the many songs of our childhood that praise her. (Despite my name, I'm not a Scot, so I'm unbiased.) Whether it's the Georgian stateliness or medieval charm of Edinburgh, the lovely rolling hills of the Borders, or the magnificent wild country of the Highlands, the Isle of Skye, the Shetlands, and the Orkneys, Scotland's rare, unspoiled beauty strikes a chord in every visitor.

Shoppers will find Scottish merchants and crafts workers delightfully entrepreneurial. Paul Phipps of Highland Stoneware says, "We accept all manner of hard currency and traveler's checks. Having a different currency will not deter a Scot from a prospective sale!"

WHAT TO BUY

Cashmere sweaters (handmade and machine-made), knitwear—especially shetland, Fair Isle, and custom-designed sweaters, cashmere and natural-fiber luxury fabric and yarns—Harris tweeds, pottery, crystal and art glass, silver jewelry, shortbread, gourmet jams and preserves (some with Scotch whiskey or Drambuie), and dolls.

Scotland

Shetland Isles

Lerwick

Orkney Isles

Kirkwall

Sanday

Western Isles

Isle of Lewis

Wick

CAITHNESS

SUTHERLAND

Lochinver

Lybster

Isle of Harris

Achnasheen

Elgin

Inverness

Isle of Skye

South Uist

Oban

Crieff

Perth

Alva

St. Andrews

Lochgilphead

Kinross

Alexandria

Falkirk

Glasgow

Edinburgh

Peebles

Galashiels

Skirling

Kelso

Hawick

Jedburgh

Langholm

KIRKCUDBRIGHTSHIRE

Kirkcudbright

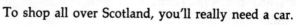

To shop all over Scotland, you'll really need a car.

1986 Currency Range

Scotland uses the British pound, but the Bank of Scotland also issues its own currency. See p. 27 for currency range.

The VAT

See p. 29.

Getting It Back

See p. 29.

Telephone Numbers

See p. 29.

Chapter 10 *Edinburgh*

Behind the cold gray stones of Edinburgh are centuries of romantic history: Mary, Queen of Scots, the poetry of Robert Burns—himself a scandalously great lover—and the sweeping novels of Sir Walter Scott. And today, often in those same historic buildings, are some of the best and most beautiful bargains in all of Scotland.

Buying knitwear is a must, and you can rationalize all your purchases on the grounds that they were great bargains that would cost hundreds of dollars more at home—and besides, Edinburgh *does* tend to be cool and damp. You'll probably wear your purchases before you get them home.

Fortunately, much of the best of Edinburgh's shopping is in a small, easily walked area, although, if you are as successful as I was, you'll need to return to your hotel two or three times a day to drop off your purchases. Happily, too, most of the outlets and shops in Edinburgh accept credit cards.

Margi Ballantine   *By appointment*
1/2 East Silver Mills Lane   *Traveler's checks in pounds,*
Edinburgh EH3 5BG   *personal checks with ID*
Tel. (031) 556 9578

Margi Ballantine's hand-painted silks unite crafts, fashion, and accessories. She makes scarves, ties, and

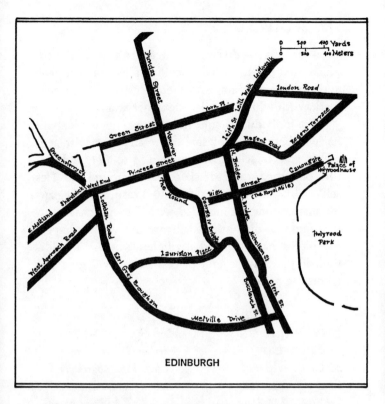

EDINBURGH

Most of Edinburgh's best shopping is in the center
of the city, on the main streets and the smaller
streets leading off them. Best bet is the Royal Mile:
High Street, the Lawnmarket, Canongate.

bow ties in crepe de chine, pongee, and twill, in a so-phisticated palette of jewel colors, plus charcoal, teal, apricot, cream, plum, and metallic silver, her trade-mark, with which she also signs her scarves.

For individual clients, Margi prices her work about halfway between wholesale and retail prices, with geo-metric scarves selling at around £14 to £24, and pic-ture-patterned scarves in six colors, at around £40. Ties sell for £17, and bow ties, for £10. Washing and clean-ing instructions are included with each purchase.

Samples, discontinued items, and slightly imper-fect pieces may be priced at wholesale or less. In addi-tion, if you buy several pieces, Margi will give you wholesale prices.

Ewe Nique Knitwear

33 Candlemaker Row
Edinburgh EH1 2QG
Tel. (031) 225 3532

Mon.–Sat. 11:00–5:30
American Express, Diners
Club, VISA/Barclaycard,
MasterCard/Access,
traveler's checks in pounds
Mail order

Ewe Nique makes high-fashion sweaters for men, women, and children and supplies Harrods and Scotch House in London and Saks Fifth Avenue and Macy's in the United States.

Ewe Nique's men's MTV jacket, a double-breasted sweater with extended shoulders, a solid shawl collar and cuffs, and a tweed-patterned body, costs £59.50. The Parallel jacket can be worn by men or women. It has a solid body and cuffs and an intricate, striking multicolor zigzag pattern on its shawl collar, double-breasted front, and sleeves. It costs £69 and comes in midnight (black), deep blue, navy, and dark gray.

For women, the Splodge shawl-collared sweater and cardigan are available for £49 and £52. The most popular color combination is a bright blue, with small motifs (splodges) of pink, red, light blue, green, and white on the bodies of the sweaters, which feature large, extended shoulders.

Children's brightly colored crewnecks feature camels, teddy bears, dogs, or tractors on navy or red backgrounds. They cost £17–£20 for sizes 20 to 26 inches, £22 for size 28 inches, £24 for size 30 inches, £27 for size 32 inches, and £29.50 for size 34 inches. Similar adults' sweaters portray dogs on red, navy, or black backgrounds, camels on navy, black, or deep blue backgrounds, and sheep on RAF blue, navy, black, red, or silver-gray backgrounds. They are available in sizes 36–46 inches (add a minimum 2 inches for ease) as vests for £29.50, as crewnecks for £39.50, and as cardigans for £42.50.

This shop has a constantly changing selection of bargains and special offers. Most recently, a variety of sweaters from earlier seasons were only £20 each, and a sweater with a brown duck motif was only £25.

Adrian Hope and Linda Lewin

Designers—Gold and Silversmiths
The Workshop
3A Henderson Place
Edinburgh EH3 5DJ
Tel. (031) 556 6432

Tues.–Sat. 9:00–5:30
VISA/Barclaycard, traveler's checks in pounds

Adrian Hope is a goldsmith, silversmith, and sculptor. Linda Lewin is a jeweler. Their work is some of the finest and most unusual in Scotland, a country where fine silver has a long tradition.

Adrian Hope's designs for the home are very sophisticated, clean-lined, elegant, and witty. African blackwood snails are £65 and £70; inlaid with ivory, their price rises to £120. Boxwood-topped, grotesque-masked silver pillboxes are priced at £265 and £285. A set of six silver demitasse spoons sells for £136. Adrian also does tiny salt spoons in sculptured laburnum-wood boxes—the perfect christening or baby gift—for £16. Other silver spoons are £23 and £32; with engraved name and date, add an additional £4–£5. More expensive silver and ebony pieces include 10-inch candlesticks for £900, an ebony-handled coffeepot for £1,200, and a matching creamer for £360.

Linda Lewin's designs range from the simplest silver snail earrings in two sizes—£23 and £25—to silver and freshwater pearl necklaces, which start at £95. The star of her collection is a £460 bridal headdress in the shape of a wreath of silver leaves adorned with pale pink freshwater pearls—obviously to become a cherished heirloom, handed down from generation to generation.

Like many artisans, Hope and Lewin will make one-of-a-kind commissioned pieces.

Maggie Belle Designs

4 Forthview
Newcraighall Road
Edinburgh EH15 3HR
Tel. (031) 669 7190

By appointment
Traveler's checks in pounds
Mail order

Maggie Belle Designs specializes in handcrafted *poupard* dolls (dolls on a stick), which originated in France in the 16th century. The wooden dolls are approximately 10 inches high, with charming hand-painted features; they are dressed individually in a wide variety of styles, including Scots tartans, traditional Scottish Country Dance, and Mary, Queen of Scots. Choose a doll dressed in traditional, ancient, or hunting tartan, with a feather-trimmed velvet tam; it costs only £4.50. The Scottish Country Dance doll is also £4.50, as is Robert Burns's muse, Clarinda, dressed in an 18th-century velvet and satin gown.

Mary, Queen of Scots, dressed in a black velvet gown and pearl-trimmed headdress with black lace veil, is £5. So is the Scottish Fishwife, who wears the traditional striped cotton or serge skirt, overskirt, and tartan headscarf and carries a fishing creel on her shoulders.

Maggie Belle also makes Wedding Belles: dolls wearing your favorite bride's wedding dress, headdress, and veil and carrying a bouquet. She uses either the original wedding-dress fabric or a close match. Send a photograph and inquiry letter for her price.

James Pringle Woollen Mill Ltd.

70–74 Bangor Road
Leith, Edinburgh EH6 5JU
Tel. (031) 553 5161/5162

Mon.–Sun. 9:00–5:00
  Oct.–Apr.; Mon.–Sun.
  9:00–5:30 May–June;
  Mon.–Sat. 9:00–6:00,
  Sun. 9:00–5:30 July–Aug.
American Express,
  VISA/Barclaycard,
  MasterCard/Access,
  traveler's checks in pounds
Mail order

Jas. Pringle Ltd. Woollen Manufacturers are in Glasgow, but their factory outlets are in Leith, an area of Edinburgh; in Inverness, in the Highlands; and in Portree, on the Isle of Skye.

Don't confuse this Pringle, Scotland's oldest tweed manufacturer, weavers since 1780, with Pringle of Scotland, the cashmere manufacturer. Pringle is a common name in Scotland. Anyway, you'll find Pringle cashmeres here, as well as Lyle & Scott, Peter Scott, and many other quality brands. Most plain women's crewneck, V-neck, and turtleneck sweaters are £70; the cardigans cost £75. Sweaters with ornate stitches and intarsias (colored patterns) are £99 and up.

The previous year's designs are better buys, of course, with women's cashmeres priced at £45 and £50, and intarsias, at £60.

Fair Isle sweaters are very inexpensive, ranging from £12.25 to £18.50; shetlands vary between £13.25 and £18.95. Aran sweaters are £32–£43, wool/mohair blends £27.50–£29.50, and lush pure mohair sweaters £38–£52—approximately half the price of designer Bernat Klein in the Scottish Borders (see 133).

Pringle's own straight skirts run £28.95; kilted tweed skirts are an exceptional buy at £26.95. For sewers, a kit containing 1 meter of wool fabric (skirt length) and enough dyed-to-match yarn to knit a sweater was a superb buy at only £10.

Topping it all off, coats of 75 percent cashmere and 25 percent wool in navy, gray, or camel are only £100, a much better buy from the standpoints of fabric quality, design, and tailoring than lower-cashmere-blend coats priced at £75.

For both sexes, pure cashmere scarves in solid colors are £28.50; scarves of 70 percent cashmere and 30 percent wool are £19.50.

One of Pringle's assets is its large men's department. Cashmere sweaters are £70–£90. Tartan jackets run approximately £80, while tartan pants (often called trews), about £40–£50. Viyella (50 percent cotton and 50 percent wool) shirts are a special buy at £18.50. Sheepskin mitts cost £7.95, and sheepskin gloves, £13.95.

Pringle also has a large children's department. These clothes are made by other designers, and they are bought up quickly, so stock is changing too constantly to write about and mention prices. However, if you're a doting parent or grandparent, look at these charming clothes.

Norman Kerr, Pringle's retail manager, likes to see his stock turn over quickly, so he always has sale racks labeled "Week's Star Buys." Absolutely anything can show up on these racks—usually at least one-third off their already low prices. It's a good idea to check these racks first before touring the rest of the store.

I feel more kindly toward the usual tourist souvenirs in the front of the shop. They are displayed well, and the selection of edible souvenirs is large, tasty, and tasteful. I'm a great fan of national delicacies, and I've brought back a good selection of honey with Drambuie (£1.95), honey with Scotch whiskey (£1.35), and marmalade with single-malt whiskey, strawberry jam with Drambuie, and peach jam with brandy (all £1.65). A good assortment of miniatures of these and other flavors was 40p each. Even if my arms never recover from schlepping all those heavy glass jars home, it was worth it!

Shortbread, in various sizes and shapes, is available, too. When shopping, remember that you're paying for the pretty picture on the tin; you may then prefer to get the basic paper packages at less than half the price (the packaging weighs less, too) and buy more goodies with your savings.

What the Scottish Craft Centre (see p. 125) is to a variety of handicrafts, the James Pringle Woollen Mill is to more commercial clothing and products: an excellent one-stop-for-everything store. There are real buys here.

Hillary Rohde
4 Carlton Street
Edinburgh EH4 1NJ
Tel. (031) 332 4147

By appointment
Traveler's checks in pounds
Mail order

I first saw Hillary Rohde's hand-knitted cashmere sweaters in Harrods about five years ago, and immediately fell in love with them for the intricacies of their cable and fancy-stitch designs. I couldn't afford them, but I fell in love with them anyway. Then I saw her sweaters in Saks, Bergdorf's, and Burberry's in New York. They were even more unaffordable, of course.

Finally, I tracked her down for this book and persuaded her to do custom work for private clients.

If you liked Hillary's black cashmere sweater splashed with enormous violet and turquoise Matisse-like flowers at Harrods, but would really love it in gray, with rust and mustard flowers, don't despair. Hillary will make it for you, and it will cost only about half its retail price. You can choose a collar from one sweater, a cable pattern from a second, a sleeve design from a third—all in about thirty colors. At her direct-to-customer prices, why not order two! For custom-made cashmeres, Hillary's prices are extremely reasonable.

Delivery time is eight to twelve weeks.

Sally's Woollies
166 High Street
Edinburgh EH1 1QS
Tel. (031) 225 1387

Mon.–Fri. 9:00–5:00; Open
only Apr. 1–Oct. 1
VISA/Barclaycard,
MasterCard/Access,
traveler's checks in pounds

If you like one of Sally Oswald's witty sweater designs, you'll probably want several. Her lamb's wool, shetland, and cotton designs are bold and bright, some with captions, and nearly all use colorful motifs. Simple batwing shapes make it possible for one size to fit sizes 32–40 inches. A few designs are straighter, with narrower sleeves, and there are a few cardigans.

Pricing is simple: £45 for shetland batwings, £50 for lamb's wool or cotton batwings and shetland cardigans, and £55 for lamb's wool cardigans. The prices here are much lower than the prices in Harrods, Selfridges, Macy's, Bloomingdale's, and B. Altman, which also carry Sally's Woollies.

Among my favorites in Sally's lamb's wool collection are Polar Bears, with vertical rows of polar bears, penguins, snowflakes, and the northern lights, and Washday Blues, with that motif in red on the left side, followed by a row of teardrops, and seven washlines holding colorful laundry covering the front of the sweater. Other amusing designs are Glitzy Ritz, with a row of crimson lipsticks being applied to crimson mouths, and Joker, in red and black, with rows of masks and jesters' heads. All are only £50.

Sally's shetland designs are equally amusing. Back at 12 uses motifs from Cinderella: rows of pumpkins, coaches, castles, mice, and the words "back at 12" on a background of dark blue. Transports of Delight shows rows of those words centered between rows of airplanes and rows of hot-air balloons. And who wouldn't want to be a Funny Bunny, with rows of yellow, turquoise, and red rabbits bordering those words on a charcoal background. All of these are only £45.

Sally's Woollies did not have mail-order service when this book went to press, but you might try phoning or writing them to check whether they have recently decided to offer this service.

Scottish Craft Centre

140 Canongate
Edinburgh EH8 8DD
Tel. (031) 556-8136/7370

Mon.–Sat. 10:00–5:30
American Express, Diners
Club, VISA/Barclaycard,
MasterCard/Access,
traveler's checks in pounds,
foreign currency

If you have time for only one shopping stop in Edinburgh, spend it here. Just make sure that you don't confuse it with the very touristy and similar-sounding Scottish Crafts, about 100 feet farther downhill on Canongate.

Started in 1949, the Scottish Craft Centre is a non-profit organization of about 330 members, of whom about 75 percent have work for sale in the shop at any time, according to Kenneth Brill, the retail manager. Nowhere in Britain have I seen such a large collection of beautiful and original work. As a bonus, a large percentage of the pieces sold here are free of VAT because they are produced in small quantities. Many are also free of U.S. customs duty because they are considered to be original works of art.

Here are some of the exciting artists and crafts workers whose designs I found unusually attractive, and their very reasonable prices.

Anne Hughes—beautiful pierced pottery. Dish in the arts-and-crafts style (the British period just before art nouveau), £30; very large platter, £55.

Judith Phibbs—enameled silver jewelry, some set with moonstones (the only gem she uses), £30–£75.

Lorraine Fernie—very classical terra-cotta stoneware. Roman-style plaques and urns, mermaid with blue-glazed tail, £35–£80. Her pieces are very heavy; fortunately, the Scottish Craft Centre ships abroad.

Mark Stanczyk—ceramics by an artist who describes himself as an "archaeologist manqué." Egyptian, Assyrian, Greek, and Roman influences are very strong in his work. Several variations on the Trojan horse in small ceramic sculptures are £45–£48.

Michelle Sanderson—textured glass plates and bowls, £20–£40.

Iva Knight—brilliantly patterned and shaped machine-knit lamb's wool sweaters, £50–£70.

Sheena Henderson—Scottish character dolls, £27.90.

June Campbell—character dolls for collectors,

such as a matron dressed in late Victorian style, including hat and pearl earrings in her pierced ears, £92.60.

Susan McKay—ceramic jewelry and buttons, perfect for summer fashions. Earrings, £4.75; matching necklace and earrings, £12.50; sets of buttons, £3.

Kathy Cumming—hand-batiked silk scarves, £18.60–£27.90, depending on the size.

Frances Sanderson—hand-printed silk scarves using Celtic motifs. Especially pretty; a Pictish princess in red and taupe, £11.15.

Roger Drew—chased silver animal pins using Celtic motifs. Eagle, boar, bull, horse, and wolf, £30; a chased silver-topped wooden bowl, £450.

Douglas Hunter—individual tiles and tile pictures. One six-tile picture, reminiscent of an art nouveau version of the famous Diane de Poitiers portrait, £80 including the frame. If you visit the Scottish Borders, make sure to stop at his studio in Ancrum (see p. 140).

Keryn Everly—beautifully colored enameled silver cuff links, £51.85; earrings, £18.35–£33.75; and decorative boxes, £93–£130.

Ola M. Gorie—silver jewelry, many of whose designs were inspired by Scotland's famed arts-and-crafts designer Charles Rennie Mackintosh. Earrings, £10.70–£15. She also makes jewelry based on Celtic and Scandinavian motifs. If you visit the Orkney Islands, stop by at her studio in Kirkwall (see p. 166).

Margery Clinton—lusterware ceramics in radiant blues. Sake cups or handleless teacups, £13.80; small square vases, £18; larger ones, slightly higher in price.

Jason Shackleton—Mediterranean-inspired folk-art candelabra. Very large blue and white fish-mobile candelabrum, £89.25; a smaller, simpler version with a dove, £32.75.

I could go on for another ten pages!

Textile Workshop and Gallery

Gladstone's Land
Lawnmarket
The Royal Mile
Edinburgh EH1 2NT
Tel. (031) 225 4570

Mon.–Sat. 10:00–4:30
Apr.–Oct.; Tues.–Sat.
10:00–4:30 Nov.–Mar.
American Express, Diners
Club, VISA/Barclaycard,
MasterCard/Access,
traveler's checks in dollars
or pounds
Mail order

Textile Workshop and Gallery specializes in designer knitwear by owner Anne Orr and other Scottish designers, in one of the oldest houses in Edinburgh, dating back to 1618.

It's difficult to find attractive patterned sweaters for men, so Textile Workshop's unisex sweaters are very welcome. A Fair Isle patterned sweater with a blue or mulberry background is £43. Iona, a crunchy textured sweater with colored dots on a navy, blue, medium gray, or mulberry background is priced at £44. Heatherstone Check, in soft tones of blue, wine, and rust shetland wool, sells for £39. Lightening Star, a dramatic shetland V-neck cardigan jacket, has a navy background, scarlet lightning and star patterns and buttons, with electric blue stripes, is £47.

Women's sweaters are very imaginative. For bold designs, Petals comes as a boat-neck sweater or a wooden-buttoned cardigan. The sweaters have unusual textured clusters of raised colored petals on backgrounds of black, natural, denim blue, or Oxford gray shetland. The sweater is £45; the cardigan, £55. Cat and Mouse is an amusing batwing sweater on which cats prowl after runaway mice in black with white, electric blue, scarlet, camel, or cerise; it costs only £35.

Feminine sweaters are here in abundance. Gypsy

Moth combines mohair and silk, with a Renaissance-style collar and cuffs, and enormous dramatic sleeves. Priced at £82, it comes in black mohair with shades of red silk, black mohair with blue and aqua silks, cream mohair with white silk, or cream mohair with soft pink silk. Silk Shale, a hand-knitted sweater, is a high-fashion version of a traditional Scottish lace pattern, with ripples of silk throughout the sweater and silk edgings on the stand-up collar and cuffs. The sweater, which comes in cream mohair with white silk, electric blue mohair with electric blue silk, scarlet mohair with scarlet silk, blue/heather mix mohair with electric blue silk, and peacock green mix mohair with turquoise silk, is £69. The same sweater sells for around £100 in London and about $200 in New York.

Don't overlook the seconds basket. Although it may contain only a dozen or so sweaters, they are only slight seconds, and the bargains are wonderful. A charming strawberry-patterned cardigan selling for £39 if perfect was only £25 as a second.

Mail-order shoppers will be delighted with the mail-order service, called the Gladstone Collection. The catalog is a group of beautifully detailed color photographs, with clear descriptions and sizes printed on the reverse of each picture. The ordering instructions are wonderfully detailed and even include requests for height and whether you would like a close-fitting or loose-fitting sweater, as well as the usual questions about bust or chest size.

THE OUTSKIRTS

Ewe Nique Knitwear

3 Lodge Street
Haddington
East Lothian EH41 3DX
Tel. (062) 082 2199

Wed.–Fri. 9:00–12:30 and 1:00–3:00, Sat. 10:00–1:00 or by appointment
American Express, Diners Club, VISA/Barclaycard, MasterCard/Access, traveler's checks in pounds
Mail order

Ewe Nique's factory shop often has more interesting sweaters at better prices than the Edinburgh outlet. If you're in the neighborhood, it's worth a visit. For a detailed description of these designer sweaters, see p. 118.

Chapter 11 *The Borders*

The Scottish Borders, for centuries the scene of battles between the English and the Scots, frequent skirmishes, and horse and cattle raids, are now the home of the fashion knitwear and textile industries, especially of cashmeres and tartans. There are many mill shops in the area, and prices are very competitive.

In addition to knitwear and textiles, the Borders are home to creators of ceramics, jewelry, crystal, and fine art glass (one-of-a-kind collectors' pieces), who have fallen in love with the beautiful countryside.

If you plan to visit the Borders in the spring or the summer, check with the towns of Galashiels, Hawick, and Jedburgh for their traditional and colorful pageants and celebrations, such as Riding the Marches in Hawick.

GALASHIELS

Peter Anderson of Scotland
Nether Mill
Huddersfield
Galashiels TD1 3BA
Tel. (0896) 2091

Mon.–Sat. 9:00–5:00 year-round; Sun. 12:00–5:00 June–Sept.
American Express, VISA/Barclaycard, MasterCard/Access, traveler's checks in pounds, personal checks with ID
Mail order

One of the things that makes Peter Anderson so special is its superb made-to-measure cashmere jackets —at the same price as ready-to-wear: only £179, including VAT. Made-to-measure cashmere skirts are £95.70, including VAT. Clothing takes about four weeks to make and is then shipped all over the world by air parcel post.

Anderson carries the world's largest range of pure worsted wool tartans—over 740 different patterns at last count!

The mill shop's sale rack has a good selection of knitwear, skirts, jackets, and capes. Cashmere sweaters run approximately £29; lamb's wool, £12. On my last trip, the sale bins held very heavy unisex cashmere crewnecks for £25–£42, and a group of merino intarsia sweaters (with knitted-in patterns) for £15.95, part of an order canceled by Nordstrom's, the posh Seattle department store. Another bin held scarves of 70 percent cashmere and 30 percent lamb's wool for only £7.95.

Gala Sheepskin Crafts

25 High Buckholmside
Galashiels
Selkirkshire TD1 2HR
Tel. (0896) 55807

Mon.–Fri. 9:30–5:30, Sat. 10:00–1:00
American Express, Diners Club, VISA/Barclaycard, MasterCard/Access, traveler's checks in pounds
Mail order

Gala Sheepskin Crafts is worth a visit for a few choice items, but only if you're in or near Galashiels. The tiny shop is not stocked well enough to rate a separate trip. It's a pity, because owner Isabel Black is friendly and helpful. However, as she says, most of her goods go to several large Scots-oriented mail-order houses in the United States.

Best bets were the charming toy leather elephants

for £10 and £15 and the children's patchwork sheepskin vests for only £9.60. The women's hats for £12.50–£18.90 were attractive, but the selection was small. Chrome-tanned sheepskins were £13.90 for seconds and £24.50 for firsts. Honestly, I couldn't see much difference.

Women's shearling mittens at £9.90 and gloves at £18.20 were lovely, but they are a better buy at James Pringle Woollen Mill in Edinburgh (see p. 121).

Bernat Klein Limited Studio Shop

High Sunderland
Galashiels
Selkirkshire TD1 3PL
Tel. (0750) 20730

Mon.–Sat. 10:00–5:00
American Express,
* VISA/Barclaycard,*
* MasterCard/Access,*
* traveler's checks in pounds*

Bernat Klein's glass-walled Architectural Association Award-winning studio was designed to show the color of his yarns and hand-knitted sweaters in true daylight. His hand-knitted sweaters use strong, subtle palettes, and are up to the minute; his sweaters of the 1960s are equally wearable and timeless.

As always, first check out the sale baskets, full of samples, discontinued models, and slight irregulars. Klein's current-season cotton or silk/cotton sweaters are £45–£60; his mohairs, £80–£110. But pure silk sweaters in the bargain baskets were only £12–£18, a silk/wool sweater was £30, and mohair sweaters, some slightly irregular, were £25–£35.

Bernat Klein is definitely worth the short detour from the main road that links the Border mill towns of Galashiels and Hawick. However, for yarns for hand knitters, I prefer visiting or mail-ordering from Texere Yarns in Bradford, England (see p. 84).

Lindean Mill Glass

Lindean Mill
Galashiels
Selkirkshire TD1 3PE
Tel. (0750) 20173

Mon.–Thurs. 9:00–6:00,
Fri.–Sat. by appointment
VISA/Barclaycard,
MasterCard/Access,
traveler's checks in pounds
Mail order

Lindean's David Kaplan is an American married to Annica Sandström, a Swede. Since 1977 they have operated a glass studio in the Scottish Borders. Their designs are in the public collections of the Glasgow Art Gallery and Museums, the Royal Scottish Museum in Edinburgh, the Turner Art Collection at Sheffield University, the Rhösska Museum in Sweden, and many other museums and galleries.

Lindean's glass falls into two categories, both of which are exquisite. One, influenced clearly by Matisse, is the one-of-a-kind museum or collector's piece —of a woman, sometimes with flowers, sometimes nude, usually in cobalt on an opaque white bowl. Price: around £200.

For daily use and display, there are white glass goblets for £10 and ruby-rimmed ones for £12. Ruby-rimmed tumblers are £4. Colored bowls are £31 and £50; with striped rims, they are £40 and £50. White glass bowls with abstract designs are £50.

Seconds are just as perfect as firsts but may be harder to match up in sets of four or more. Goblets are around half price—only £5 to £7—as are small colored bowls—only £17.

Don't worry about carrying your purchases all over Scotland; Lindean Mill Glass will ship them home for you. If they are one-of-a-kind pieces (even the abstracts), they will be duty-free because they are considered by U.S. customs to be works of art by a living artist.

Charles N. Whillans
The Knitwear Shop
Channel Street
Galashiels
Selkirkshire TD1
Tel. (0896) 55554

Mon.–Tues. and Thurs.–Sat.
9:00–5:00, Wed.
9:00–1:00
American Express,
VISA/Barclaycard,
MasterCard/Access,
traveler's checks in pounds
Mail order

See p. 135 for a complete write-up of the main shop, located in Hawick, which has longer hours and more merchandise.

HAWICK

Valerie Louthan
Limited
2 Kirk Wynd
Hawick TD9 0AL
Tel. (0450) 78000

Mon.–Fri. 1:00–4:00
American Express,
VISA/Barclaycard,
MasterCard/Access,
traveler's checks in pounds,
U.S. dollars
Mail order—capes only

Valerie Louthan's exciting, sophisticated cashmere designs for both men and women are sold by Gucci, Nina Ricci, Givenchy, and Christian Dior, but they are far more affordable at her new mill shop, opened in mid-June 1986. Since the shop is quite new, telephone before you visit to see whether business hours have been expanded.

This mill shop sells at cost a mixture of canceled orders, samples, and slight seconds, some with matching skirts and trousers; consequently, the prices are considerably lower than wholesale prices. For example, Louthan's classic Benita cape, which sells for £460 in

Britain and "a minimum of $600 in the United States," according to Louthan, is priced between £100 and £160 for slight seconds at the mill shop, depending on quality. Her colors are mouth-watering:

Black	Praline	Wine	Caramel
Tartan	Viola	Dark navy	Emerald
green	Nile (green)	Silver	Ruby
Gunmetal	Sapphire	Sandstone	Mimosa
Natural	White	Peach	(yellow)
String			

Sweaters for men and women, which can cost as much as £420 in London's posh Burlington Arcade, sell for £50–£150 here. Dresses in fashionable shapes that never become outdated range from around £100 to £200. Valerie Louthan is a must-visit for shoppers who demand more from their cashmeres than classic simple good looks.

Tom Scott Knitwear Manufacturer

Thorncroft
Denholm
Hawick
Roxburghshire TD9 8NJ
Tel. (045) 087283

Easter-Christmas: Mon.–Fri.
10:00–12:00 and
2:00–4:30, Sat.
2:00–4:30
VISA/Barclaycard,
MasterCard/Access,
traveler's checks in pounds
Mail order

Sweaters for men, women, and children in cashmere, lamb's wool, and shetland are made and sold here. Cashmeres are £39.50 and £47 and come in 26 colors. Among Tom Scott's hand-knitted patterns are argyles, stripes, rosebuds, and abstracts—all priced according to the complexity of design, all priced far below retail.

Make sure you check the sale rack, which often has cashmeres for as little as £25 and shetlands for as low as £5.

The Weensland Spinning Company

Weensland Mills
Hawick TD9 9RJ
Tel. (0450) 72509

Mon.–Fri. 9:00–12:30,
*   1:30–5:00*
Traveler's checks in pounds,
*   U.S. dollars*
Mail order

Weensland produces cashmere and top-quality lamb's wool yarns, which can be used by home knitters. Although Weensland sells primarily to industrial users and has no mail-order catalog facilities, private customers who are familiar with Weensland's yarns can order them by mail. Prices for the 19 shades of cashmere in hand-knitter's 3-ply yarn range from £70.75–£75.50 per kilogram for dark shades to £75.00–£87.40 per kilogram for medium shades to £99–£104 per kilogram for light shades. (*Note:* You should be able to knit two to four adult sweaters from 1 kilogram of cashmere yarn.)

Even more attractive are the "odd lot" yarn prices: £50 per kilogram for dark shades, £65 per kilogram for medium shades, and £80 per kilogram for light colors. As W. W. Henderson, Weensland's general sales manager, says, "If the customer is prepared to knit at home to her own pattern, she is going to come up with a beautifully handling cashmere sweater at prices much cheaper than in the London or New York stores for similar quality."

Hand-knitter's 3-ply lamb's wool yarn has only two sets of prices for its 14 colors: £14 per kilogram regular price, £10 per kilogram "odd lot" price.

Charles N. Whillans
The Knitwear Shop
Teviotdale Mills
Hawick TD9 7BR
Tel. (0450) 73128/73311

Mon.–Sat. 9:00–5:15
American Express,
*   VISA/Barclaycard,*
*   MasterCard/Access,*
*   traveler's checks in pounds*
Mail order

Charles N. Whillans is an outlet for local knitwear factories that do not sell to the public—for example, Pringle, Braemar, Lyle & Scott, Peter Scott, and Glenhowe.

The shop, which is about 100 feet long, has large tables down each side, on which discontinued designs and slight seconds are displayed according to size. One table is a display of ladies' cashmere sweaters starting at £30; another has men's cashmeres from £35. Owner Charles Whillans comments: "I also have large baskets which were previously used in the factories, and these are regularly filled with cheaper clearing lines. Customers seem to enjoy searching for a bargain."

And right he is! The sale bins had one-of-a-kind sweaters, often in small sizes, for £9.95. Other bins housed shetland sweaters for only £6.95.

Sale racks (they call them rails in the United Kingdom) are treasure troves, too. Pringle wool worsted skirts in pastels for spring were £15.75, and a few slightly imperfect cashmere skirts were only £15. Kilted skirts were priced at £19.95 and £24.50.

The men's department is nearly as large as the women's. Cashmere V-neck sweaters are £59.95; crewnecks or turtlenecks, £69.95 (some of lesser quality are £39.95); and two-ply cashmere intarsias (with knitted-in patterns), £85 and £89.

Whillans does a large mail-order business. New brochures are mailed every September, and special-sale brochures are sent out in February. Both are available all year on request. Telephone orders are accepted with credit cards.

White of Hawick
Victoria Road
Hawick TD9 7AH
Tel. (0450) 73206

Mon.–Sat. 9:00–5:15
VISA/Barclaycard,
*   MasterCard/Access*
Mail order

While not a mill shop, White carries cashmere and lamb's wool garments made by such top designers as Lyle & Scott and Peter Scott, many of whom restrict their mill shops to their employees. White's own garments are made by Lyle & Scott and other manufacturers. Ladies' cashmere pullovers and V-neck sweaters are £37.95; cardigans are £42.95 and £46.95. Ladies' shetland and Fair Isle sweaters are only £13.50, and the lamb's wool sweaters vary between £16.95 and £18.95. Men's cashmere sweaters are priced at £34.95 for single-ply, and £45.95 and £52.95 for two-ply. Men's lamb's wool sweaters range from £16.95 to £23.95; and lightly oiled Breton and Guernsey sweaters, from £14.95 to £19.95.

White's color range is superb. Some women's sweaters come in 22 colors.

Labeling is very important here. "Slight imperfects" are marked, and the staff will point out the imperfections to you. A more valuable designation is "special offer," which means that the garment is perfect but is a canceled order or discontinued design. Many of these are reduced to below cost, like a cashmere cardigan in the previous year's color reduced from £65 to £37.

The best buys in cashmere are in the front window and in the big cardboard boxes, marked by size, beneath them. On a recent trip, all violet sweaters, including intarsias (with knitted-in patterns), were only £25. Other bargains: a Johnston's of Elgin yellow crewneck for £29.95, a Lyle & Scott gray turtleneck for £37.95, a cobalt cashmere cardigan for £43, and some intarsia crewnecks in a 90-percent cashmere and 10-percent silk blend (marvelous spring weight!) for £38.95.

Lamb's wool sweaters are excellent buys, too. For men, Johnston's of Elgin sweaters are £16.95 if perfect and £10.95 if slightly imperfect. Johnston's women's lamb's wools are £14.95 and £15.95 if perfect and only £8.95 if slightly imperfect.

JEDBURGH

Douglas Hunter Ceramic Tile

By appointment
Traveler's checks in pounds

Woodland Centre
Harestanes
Ancrum
Jedburgh
Roxburghshire TD8 6UQ
Tel. (08353) 328

One of Douglas Hunter's tiled pictures that I saw at the Scottish Craft Centre in Edinburgh was so charming that I went out to the Borders to visit his studio and see more of his work.

Douglas Hunter is an artist-craftsman who produces hand-painted tile pictures and ceramic murals. Much of his work is executed in the traditional tube-lining technique, in which areas of colored glazes are separated by a very fine outline of clay that has been piped onto the surface of a plain tile. Used on its own or combined with other forms of pottery painting, tube-lining produces a very rich range of colors and excellent detail.

Hunter is clearly influenced by the work of Aubrey Beardsley and early art nouveau. His studio prices are much closer to wholesale than to retail. A delightful four-tile plaque of a mermaid luring a fish was only £22. My favorite, a 12-tile picture of the Three Graces, was around £150, depending on whether it was framed.

Do look at his single tiles and seconds—as low as £1 or £2 each.

Hunter does a great deal of commission work, so you can choose your own subject or design when you discuss your own requirements.

KELSO

Norman Cherry
Woodmarket Gallery
36–38 Woodmarket
Kelso
Roxburghshire TD5
Tel. (0573) 24032

Mon.–Tues., Thurs.–Sat.
10:30–5:30, Wed.
10:00–12:30
Traveler's checks in pounds

Norman Cherry is a contemporary wirework and fused-wire jeweler whose designs won him a Churchill Scholarship to study abroad. One of his comet brooches was used for a major crafts exhibition in 1986.

Typical of his work: a triangular silver pendant, £41; a silver caddy spoon with a geometric handle, £35; geometric-gridded silver earrings, £20; a small wooden serving spoon inlaid with silver, £25; and a silver and colored titanium pendant of a cat sitting in a window with a flowerpot, £57. Delicate gold rings, some set with semiprecious stones, sell for £50–£70, and oval woven-gold earrings, for £35.

Sandra Smith, Cherry's partner, has an unusual collection of silver chignon or scarf pins for £20–£25; with gold added, the price rises to £35. Earrings in silver, oxidized to highlight design elements, are £20 for a spiral design and £23 for acorns. Best bet: a silver brooch of a cottage, in great detail, for £45. Sandra will undertake commissions to make brooches copying your house or apartment building. For a quotation, send a photograph with your letter.

The Woodmarket Gallery also sells charming wooden puzzles made up of groups of animals for £4–£10.

Unfortunately, this delightful shop does not yet accept credit cards. Phone ahead to find out whether this policy has changed, or bring lots of cash or traveler's checks. Otherwise, like me, you'll leave empty-handed, wishing that you had.

Francine Dunkley
70 The Linn
Kelso
Roxburghshire TD5 8EY
Tel. (0573) 25159

By appointment
Traveler's checks in pounds,
  personal checks with ID
Mail order

Francine Dunkley creates beautiful hand-knitted designs that she sells primarily as kits, although she does do some custom knitting. She specializes in finding unusual natural yarns and combining them in her designs. One lovely sweater—Venezia, an abstract of bridges and their reflections in the water—used navy alpaca as a main color and a yarn blending 40 percent silk, 40 percent wool, and 20 percent kid mohair in lustrous jewel tones. The price for the kit, containing all the yarn a knitter would need, instructions, a charted graph, and a color photograph of the finished sweater, is around £40, depending on the size. In pure wool, the price is around £28.

Francine also sells luxury yarns alone, without her exclusive designs. For yarn samples and brochures, send $4 if you live in the United States or £1 if you live in Britain. Either amount is refundable on your first order, and there are discounts of 5 percent on orders over £50 and of 8 percent on orders over £80.

Francine's prices are excellent—for example, about £1.40 per 50 grams (35 percent) cheaper for a pure alpaca yarn than at Littlewoods, a large British chain of stores. In addition, her comments on each yarn are quite helpful. About alpaca, her price list says, "The structure of alpaca fibre is similar to that of wool but is softer, more lustrous and has a much better resistance to pilling, qualities which are making alpaca increasingly popular. Knits as 4 ply, approx. 200 meters per 50 grams, 3mm needles, from 350 grams for a 34" sweater."

If you visit Francine and you are lucky, you may find some beautiful samples and discontinued models for £50 to £70. They are well worth the price.

KINROSS AND KINROSS-SHIRE

Jacqui Seller   *By appointment*
Ceramic Design   *Traveler's checks in pounds,*
"Lynallan"   *personal checks with ID*
Main Street
Kinnesswood
Kinross-shire KY13 7HN
Tel. (059) 284 638

Jacqui Seller's charming pierced and carved ceramic giftware, decorated with flowers and butterflies, includes boxes, vases, mirrors, ceramic and velvet pincushions (called pin boxes), pomanders, wall plates, and napkin rings. Retail prices in Britain range from £2 to £25. At the designer's showroom, however, prices of discontinued designs and slight seconds vary from only £1 to a little over £12.

At Seller's showroom, pomanders are £4.20 for the

daisy motif, £5.25 for the pimpernel or pansy, £5.80 for the sweet pea, and £6.30 for the rose. Potpourri in Rose Garden, Evening Garden, or Lavender fragrance is only 26p per ½ ounce.

Pin boxes are £4.20 for the daisy motif, £5.25 for the pansy, £6.30 for the sweet pea, £4.75 for the small rose, and £5.80 for the larger rose. Butterfly napkin rings are £1 each and £6.45 for the boxed set of six. Standing or hanging mirrors, in bluebell, fuchsia, rose, and sweet-pea designs, range from £7.35 to £12.10, and vases in four shapes and seven floral motifs vary between £4.70 and £9.45.

Todd & Duncan Mill Shop

Kinross KY13 7DH
Tel. (0577) 63521
Mon.–Fri.
(0577) 63528 Sat.

Mon.–Sat. 9:00–5:00
Apr.–Sept. and Dec.; other
months, closed Thurs.
American Express, Diners
Club, VISA/Barclaycard,
MasterCard/Access,
traveler's checks in pounds

Todd & Duncan is one of the subsidiaries of Dawson International, the parent company of Ballantyne, Pringle, McGeorge, and many other exclusive designer labels whose samples and overstocks wind up here. The elegant Ballantyne cashmere sweater with beautiful hand-knitted flowers that is £200–£250 at Harrods and $500–$600 in the United States is only £70–£80 here, but it may be only one-of-a-kind. Todd & Duncan cashmere yarn for hand knitting is sometimes available, too, in quantities much smaller than you'd otherwise have to order.

Merchandise is carried in breadth rather than depth, and turnover is rapid, so it's hard to predict what will be in stock, but the bargains are so great that the store is always worth a visit.

PEEBLES

Robert Noble & Co. Ltd.

Mon.–Fri. 9:30–4:00
Traveler's checks in pounds

March Street Mills
Peebles EH45 8ER
Tel. (0721) 20146

Robert Noble's weaving mill is one of the best sources of designer fabric in the Border Country. No surprise—it's been making fine cloth since 1666. A skirt length of superb first-quality black and white herringbone cashmere cost £10 here, £60 per meter in London, and over $100 per yard in New York. Slightly irregular cashmere fabric is even less—£7.50 per meter.

Noble also makes cashmere scarves, 60-inch-wide worsteds, Scottish tweeds, and silk/wool blends, all available, from time to time, in the mill shop for around £4–£10 per meter. At these prices, a woman can make herself a cashmere suit for around $80, including lining and buttons. Price at Saks Fifth Avenue? Over $1,000.

Chapter 12 *Glasgow and Environs*

There are a few—but quite good—places to shop in and around Glasgow, which is only an hour's drive from Edinburgh. Accordingly, this is a small chapter, but it rated being separated from Chapter 14, "The Rest of Scotland," because it is so near Edinburgh.

If you do visit Glasgow, make sure to see the work of Charles Rennie Mackintosh, who was to Scotland what William Morris was to England: a designer of furniture, fabric, and all beautiful things.

GLASGOW CITY

Antartex Ltd.
127 Buchanan Street
Glasgow
Tel. (041) 204 1167

Mon.–Sat. 9:00–5:30
American Express,
*   VISA/Barclaycard,*
*   MasterCard/Access,*
*   traveler's checks in*
*   pounds*
Mail order

See p. 148 for a complete write-up of the main shop, located in Alexandria. Both shops carry approximately the same quantity of merchandise, though specific items may vary slightly.

Saltoun Pottery/Quantum Ceramics

Saltoun Lane
24 Ruthven Street
Glasgow G2
Tel. (041) 334 4240

Tues.–Sat. 9:30–5:30
VISA/Barclaycard,
MasterCard/Access
Mail order

Saltoun's pottery and ceramics are sold by the Design Centre in London and by Conran's—at much higher prices, of course. Among Saltoun's most popular products are minimalist-design vases in solid black, solid white, white with black check, square grid, gray check, black with white check or gold check. They range from £9.50 to £17.50, depending on the size. As a bonus, these vases in porcelain are the same price as they are in earthenware. Slight seconds start at only £4.95.

Sets of six mugs, creamer, and sugar bowl in beige with a single abstract brown fuchsia blossom are only £17.50; with matching coffeepot, £26.50. Other glazes and patterns are available or can be special-ordered.

Saltoun's ginger-jar-shaped pastel-abstract (their term is "sugar almond") lamp bases come in four sizes, priced from about £22 to £55. Miniature versions of this shape, which become perfume bottles, sell for £4.95 (£5.95 if with gold luster). When slightly imperfect, they sell for £3.95 and are ideal as bud vases.

Multiple orders will be charged wholesale prices, which are even lower than those shown above.

LOMOND INDUSTRIAL ESTATE— DUMBARTONSHIRE

Antartex Ltd.
Lomond Industrial Estate
Alexandria
Dumbartonshire G83 0TP
Tel. (0389) 52393

Mon.–Sat. 9:00–5:30, Sun.
  10:00–5:00
American Express,
  VISA/Barclaycard,
  MasterCard/Access,
  traveler's checks in
  pounds
Mail order

Lovers of fine shearling and suede who were disappointed when Antartex closed its Madison Avenue shop in New York several years ago will be delighted to find the Antartex factory shop and its Glasgow outlet. Men's shearling jackets range from around £149 to £179, and ladies', from £131 to £162, including VAT. Coats are about £190–£220. Other good buys are sheepskin and shearling moccasins, slippers, gloves, and hats. Adorable shearling baby booties are less than £2.50. Sheepskin rugs come in many sizes and in a variety of colors and prices. They've been used by every British antarctic survey team since 1955, and are a lovely small luxury for your toes every winter morning.

The Antartex factory shop always carries several racks of samples and discontinued items, but merchandise moves too quickly to describe—except to say that the prices are even lower than those mentioned above.

**Lomondside
Knitwear Ltd.**
Lomond Industrial Estate
Alexandria
Dumbartonshire G83 0TP
Tel. (0389) 52517

*Mon.–Fri. 9:00–5:00, Sat.
9:30–5:00, Sun.
10:30–5:00 in Apr.–Oct.
and 11:30–5:00 in
Nov.–Mar.*
*American Express, Diners
Club, VISA/Barclaycard,
MasterCard/Access,
traveler's checks in pounds*

Lomondside is a small company that produces good solid-color cashmere and lamb's wool sweaters. Its factory shop also carries Aran and mohair knits made by its cottage-industry hand knitters. Women's cashmeres are £39.50–£44, and men's, £41–£55. Lamb's wool sweaters are £18–£20, hand-knitted mohairs £44–£49, and hand-knitted Aran sweaters £30–£45, depending on the size and complexity of design.

Women's prepleated wool kilted-skirt kits (just attach the waistband and the leather fastenings) cost £26.90; pure wool skirt lengths sell for £6.90.

Best stocking stuffers are the cashmere dickeys for only £7—perfect under open shirts and sweaters.

There's a lot of tourist merchandise here, but also some decent things at good prices.

Chapter 13 *The Highlands and Islands*

ღვჯვჯვჯ

For spectacular scenery and unusual wildlife, Scotland's Highlands and islands—(Skye, the Shetlands, the Orkneys, and hundreds more)—are unmatched. The islands are also a treasure trove of archaeological finds—Neolithic, Celtic, and Viking—which inspire local artists and crafts workers.

Whether crafts workers move to the Highlands and islands because they love the country and are inspired by its beauty or whether they are born there and their artistic tastes are formed by their surroundings is unimportant. What *is* important for us is that there are many rare and unusual bargains in these beautiful and secluded parts of Scotland.

THE HIGHLANDS

ACHNASHEEN

Aultbea Toys
32 Mellon Charles
Aultbea
Achnasheen
Ross-shire IV22 2JL
Tel. (044) 582400

Mon.–Fri. 9:30–5:30, Sat. 10:00–5:00; also by appointment
VISA/Barclaycard
Mail order: send order without payment, stating whether you prefer airmail or surface delivery, and Aultbea will quote total price, including postage

Valerie Brown's delightful soft plush toys are entirely handmade. Prices are as much as 50 percent below retail and range from £1.50 to £18. The fuzzy white lamb costs £4.25 and is a very popular baby gift, as are the small rabbits for £5.50. Small smiling teddy bears are also £5.50. For older children, a fox comes as a pajama case as well as a soft toy for £18, and a cat comes either way for £12.

Adults prefer Aultbea's dogs. Extremely lifelike Yorkshire terriers, which are often taken for the real thing, are £18, as are black Scottish terriers and West Highland White terriers. Dopey Dog, whose color is like an Irish setter's and whose expression is lovably foolish, costs £12.50.

Most unusual are Aultbea's Highland wildlife toys. Puffins with striped red, yellow, and blue beaks are £7.50; mallard ducks, £9; and blue-eyed baby seals in gray, fawn, or white, £8.50. A mole wearing a tartan vest is very popular and is only £5.50. Ms. Brown will try to supply the tartan of your choice whenever possible.

Because all toys are one of a kind, Ms. Brown will consider special requests.

ARGYLL

Caithness Glass PLC

Oban Glassworks
Lochavullan Estate
Oban
Argyll
Tel. (0631) 63386

Mon.–Fri. 9:00–5:00; Sat.
in summer 9:00–1:00
American Express, Diners
Club, VISA/Barclaycard,
MasterCard/Access,
traveler's checks in pounds

This factory outlet is only a five-minute walk south of the railroad station. See p. 185 for a complete write-up of the main shop, located in Perth, which has the best shopping hours, including Sundays.

Flora MacDonald
21 Airds Crescent
Oban
Argyll
Tel. (0631) 65281

By appointment, including
*   evenings and weekends*
Traveler's checks in pounds
Mail order

Flora MacDonald designs hand-knitted sweaters for men and women, some from hand-spun, hand-dyed yarn. Designs range from the traditional warm, functional Scottish sweaters to luxury garments of mohair, silk, alpaca, and cashmere.

A geometric dolman-sleeved sweater in black, gray, red, and white, with a detachable tube hood, in a mohair/wool blend is only £40. An alpaca sweater with unusual cabled panels is available in black/cream/pale gray or brown/cream/beige for £75. A wonderful hand-knitted 1940s-style cardigan with knitted shoulder pads, belt, and buttons comes in black, beige, or cream and is also £75. Given the price of white cashmere yarn, Flora MacDonald's white cashmere and white silk ribbed classic sweater is a best buy at only £80.

One-of-a-kind evening sweaters in cashmere, silk, or mohair—from about £50 to £100—use lace stitches in oyster, fern, and wave motifs, and are embroidered with pearls, antique crystal beads, or striking copper rivets and are threaded with velvet or satin ribbons. You can create your own design and have it knitted up and sent to you.

Best of the men's sweaters are a hand-knitted guernsey in cream Aran wool for £55 and a unisex hand-knitted double-breasted jacket in Icelandic or Aran wool in light gray/navy or cream/brown for £48.

Knap Studio
Lochgilphead
North Knapdale
Argyll PA31 8PS
Tel. (054685) 209

By appointment
Any form of currency

Knap Studio's Elizabeth Lorimer works in two media—both beautifully and very inexpensively.

Folklore-inspired stained-glass panels, ready to hang, are only £5 for the 7- by 5-inch size and £4 for the 4- by 5-inch size. The larger panels are quite detailed; one favorite piece shows a woman in a crimson cloak holding a deer, against a background of night sky, a crescent moon, and a single star. The smaller panels often depict Viking ships, flowers, birds, or animals.

Mrs. Lorimer's watercolor paintings are also inspired by folklore. They possess a dreamlike quality caused by figures and objects floating or being superimposed on each other. Two favorites—now sold, although similar ones are available—are a painting of a young woman playing the harp in a forest, surrounded by an ibex, a swan, and two ghostly figures, and a painting of a Viking ship, with a bird partly obscuring the sail and the sun and with a heroically large Viking chief in the foreground. These watercolors, up to 20 by 30 inches, sell for only £40 to £60—a rare bargain.

CAITHNESS

Caithness Glass PLC
Harrowhill
Wick
Caithness
Tel. (0955) 2286

Mon.–Fri. 9:00–5:00, Sat. 9:00–1:00; Sat. in summer 9:00–4:00
American Express, Diners Club, VISA/Barclaycard, MasterCard/Access, traveler's checks in pounds

See p. 185 for a complete write-up of the main store, located in Perth, which has the best shopping hours, including Sundays.

North Nor East Designs

Newlands of Forse
Lybster
Caithness KW3 6BX
Tel. (05934) 337

By appointment
Traveler's checks in pounds,
foreign currency
Mail order

Lawrence Message makes silver jewelry in this small workshop. He fabricates his designs from sheet silver, so they are lightweight but quite strong.

Among his most attractive designs are earrings in the shape of an outlined apple for £7.50, £8, and £9. His frog pins and brooches are clever and unusual, ranging from £6.30 to £15.25, depending on the size and intricacy.

My favorite is his Wave pendant, a contemporary design of silver wires that gives a feeling of vigorous movement within an open rectangular frame. Complete with attached chain, it is one of his most expensive pieces, at £48.

INVERNESS AND INVERNESS-SHIRE

Deirdre Minogue Knitwear

"The Shop"
Drumnadrochit
Inverness-shire
Tel. (045) 6204

Mon.–Sat. 9:00–5:30
year-round; evenings
8:00–10:00 and Sun.
11:00–5:30 June–Aug.;
also by appointment
VISA/Barclaycard,
MasterCard/Access,
traveler's checks in pounds,
foreign currency
Mail order

Deirdre Minogue works primarily in shetland yarn to design her beautiful, elaborate sweaters. At £30 to £120, her sweaters and jackets are expensive—but worth it. Her current collection is inspired by the intricate patterns and colors of Persian and Oriental carpets and demonstrates the richness possible in knitting patterns.

Deirdre Minogue's Gendje Carpet sweater is a boat-neck style, available with either batwing or standard sleeves. It comes in Tourmaline/Peacock (a sage green/turquoise/orange combination), Cavatina/Heather (moss green/wine/beige), and Grape/Goodwood (violet/pink/turquoise) and costs £58. The Gendje Carpet design is also available as a hip-length jacket for £84.

Her Kashmir sweater is an Indian carpet design translated to a double-breasted, shawl-collared jacket with pockets and elaborate borders. In comes in a red and wild rose combination or a moorit (a greenish brown) and rust combination for £84; it also comes as a batwing sweater with a round or V neck for £58.

Mosaic is an unusual sweater with an interesting diagonal pattern in both front and back. Made of either shetland or botany wool, it suits both men and women and comes in plum/gray, black/blue, or gray/white for £58.

There is usually a selection of samples, one-of-a-kinds, and discontinued designs available at excellent prices.

Jas. Pringle Ltd.
Holm Woollen Mill
Inverness
Tel. (0463) 223311

Mon.–Fri. 8:30–6:00, Sat.
9:00–5:30, Sun.
10:00–5:00 Apr.–Oct.;
Mon.–Fri. 9:00–6:00,
Sat. 9:00–5:00 Nov.–Mar.
American Express, Diners
Club, VISA/Barclaycard,
MasterCard/Access,
traveler's checks in all
currencies
No mail order, but will ship
your purchases

See p. 121 for a complete write-up of the main store, located in Edinburgh.

SUTHERLAND

**Highland
  Stoneware
  Limited**
Lochinver
Sutherland IV27 4LP
Tel. (05714) 376

*Mon.–Fri. 9:00–6:00
  Nov.–Mar.; Mon.–Sat.
  9:00–6:00 Apr.–Oct.; also
  by appointment*
*VISA/Barclaycard,
  MasterCard/Access,
  traveler's checks in pounds
  and U.S. dollars, foreign
  currency*
Mail order

Highland Stoneware's patterns are as cheerful and charming as its owners. The tableware, cookware, and giftware are designed with flair and humor, taking their inspiration from Highland wildlife, landscapes, and seascapes—all hand-painted, with no two pieces exactly alike.

Many patterns in this stoneware, which goes from freezer to microwave, coordinate. A flock of sheep scatter over cookware casseroles, mixing bowls, and soufflé dishes; the same sheep gambol over giftware mugs, cheese dishes, and decorative plates, with a Highland landscape in the background. The witty Hens and Cockerels pattern, available in both cookware and giftware, features hens on tightropes, with umbrellas, striped socks, and ballet shoes. The Sea Landscape giftware pattern is as beautiful and serene as the Highlands it depicts.

The prettiest tableware patterns are Celadon Floral, which resembles the old Stangl patterns of the 1940s and 1950s, and Culkein, a deceptively simple blue and white pattern that could be taken for the best Scandinavian, Japanese, or Rosenthal ceramics.

Prices for Highland Stoneware's handmade, hand-painted stoneware are very reasonable. Slight seconds —sold only here and at Highland Stoneware's branch shop in nearby Ullapool (see p. 157)—are approximately one-third lower than Scottish retail prices and less than half of U.S. prices for similar stoneware. The Sea Landscape large fruit bowl is £22.50 here, and £29.50 in Edinburgh; the Sea Landscape 10-inch plate is £14.95 here and £19.25 in Edinburgh.

In the Hens and Cockerels pattern, a 5-pint casserole is £29.50 here and £45 at retail, as is the 14-inch oval baker. A set of 2- and 1-pint spouted bowls sells for £20.50 here and £30.75 at retail, while the individual soufflé dishes cost £3.25 here and £4.50 at retail. A five-piece place setting of Celadon Floral is priced at £19 here and £29 elsewhere, and a five-piece place setting of Culkein is £16.35 here and £24.50 elsewhere.

Besides all these items, Highland Stoneware also sells some newer pieces as part of market testing and some special pieces that are available only at the factory. Most interesting were some long, flat, fish-shaped salmon servers, designed for the catering trade but perfect for home entertaining and for gifts. These, sold retail at around £35–£40, were available here for £23–£27.

ULLAPOOL

Highland Stoneware Limited
Mill Street
Ullapool IV26 2UN
Tel. (0854) 2980

Mon.–Fri. 9:00–6:00 Nov.–Mar.; Mon.–Sat. 9:00–6:00 and by appointment
VISA/Barclaycard, MasterCard/Access, traveler's checks in pounds and U.S. dollars, foreign currency
Mail order

Highland Stoneware, whose main workshop is in nearby Lochinver, Sutherland (see above), makes its vases here. Prices for slight seconds—sold only at Highland Stoneware—are approximately one-third less than Scottish retail prices and less than half of comparable U.S. prices. Cylindrical vases are priced at £8.95, £14.05, and £24.50 in the tranquil Sea Landscape pattern here and £13.50, £22.50, and £36.75 at retail. Round vases in Sea Landscape, which retail for £10.50 and £13.50, sell for £6.95 and £8.95 here. Prices for vases in the Varied Floral pattern, which celebrates Highland flowers, are slightly lower.

THE ISLANDS

ISLE OF LEWIS

Clansman Mill Shop
30 Newton Street
Stornoway
Isle of Lewis PA87 2RW
Tel. (0851) 3065

Mon.–Sat. 9:00–6:00
American Express,
VISA/Barclaycard,
MasterCard/Access,
traveler's checks in pounds,
personal checks with ID
Will mail orders placed at the shop

Clansman makes glorious handwoven Harris tweeds in three weights, all 28–29 inches wide: 10–11 ounces, 8–9 ounces, and 6–7 ounces per yard. Depending on the weight, they cost £5–£5.50 per yard. In addition to the more common black/white and brown/white herringbones, there are some dazzling herringbone patterns in black/violet, black/aqua, and bright orange/charcoal brown—ideal for women's suits or for skirts and matching stoles. Other plaids and tweeds, in bright or subtle colors, are wonderful for either men or women, and a few solid colors, like marigold, light blue, and coral, could make spring blazers for men and women or spring suits for women.

Exquisite knitting yarn matches the Harris tweed fabric. The 3-ply yarn is sold in hanks of 8 ounces for £3.75 per pound. (An average man's sweater takes 40 ounces; a woman's, 32 ounces.) Colors are glowing and jewel-like, or subtle and heathery. Although there are no kits that combine skirt-length fabric and knitting yarn, it's probably just as well. You'll have more fun coordinating yarn and fabric yourself.

Stornoway Pottery Ltd.

Borve Pottery
Borve
Isle of Lewis PA86 0RX
Tel. (085185) 345

Mon.–Sat. 9:30–6:00;
*   evenings by appointment*
Traveler's checks in pounds
Mail order

Stornoway is a small pottery enterprise. Husband and wife Alex and Sue Blair make all the pots themselves. The vast majority are hand-thrown on a potter's wheel; occasional pieces are handcrafted by other techniques. Many of the pieces are signed, dated, and impressed with Stornoway's own mark. The Blairs make a wide range of pots, cups, saucers, mugs, plates, and bowls, as well as lamp bases, vases, planters, and decorative bowls.

The glazes are quite varied: from a soft gray-blue usually combined with a rich *tenmoku* (a dark brown glaze, originally from Japan), which captures some of the atmosphere of the Isle of Lewis, to bright reds and deep burgundies to a rich and subtle chun (medium) blue.

Large plates (approximately 11 inches) sell for around £18, and small plates (approximately 6 inches), for around £8. Large serving bowls are priced at about

£20, and lamp bases, at £18–£40. Planters start at £9.50; vases begin at £7.

ISLE OF SKYE

Edinbane Pottery
Edinbane
Isle of Skye
Inverness-shire IV51 9PW
Tel. (047082) 234

Mon.–Fri. 9:00–6:00
mid-Sept.–mid-June;
Mon.–Sat. 9:00–6:00
mid-June–mid-Sept.; also by
appointment
American Express,
VISA/Barclaycard,
MasterCard/Access,
traveler's checks in pounds,
personal checks by
arrangement
Mail order

Stuart Whatley's Edinbane Pottery makes a wide range of functional and decorative wood-fired stoneware, tableware, and pots, many of which are salt-glazed. Visitors can often watch Whatley throwing, turning, glazing, and firing pieces in his workshop, as well as see the finished pieces in his showroom.

A stoneware dinner set in cream bordered with rust features small, medium, and large plates for £3, £5, and £8, a large salad bowl for £18, individual salad/cereal/fruit bowls for £3.50, small and large pitchers for £7.50 and £16, and mugs for £3.

Tap jars—antique containers for whiskey, with a cork at the top and a spigot at the bottom—start at £25 for a blue, rust, and gray salt-glazed design. Matching small goblets are £4.

Lamp bases are charming and unusual. A large globe in brown-speckled beige that resembles a giant bird's egg is only £18. Smaller conical designs in blue and rust on a cream background are £12.

If you knit, sew, or simply like to give your clothes a designer touch, look at Edinbane's pottery buttons, which start at only 40p.

Jas. Pringle Ltd.
Skye Woollen Mill Ltd.
Portree
Isle of Skye
Tel. (0478) 2889

Mon.–Sat. 9:00–5:30 week before Easter–Oct. 31; Sun. 11:00–4:00 week before Easter–Sept. 30

American Express, Diners Club, VISA/Barclaycard, MasterCard/Access, traveler's checks in all currencies

No mail order, but will ship your purchases

See p. 121 for a complete write-up of the main store, located in Edinburgh.

Skye Crotal Knitwear
Camus Chros
Duisdeal
Isle of Skye IV43 8QR
Tel. (04713) 271

Mon.–Thurs. 8:30–5:30, Fri. 8:30–5:00, Sat. 9:00–1:00, 2:00–4:00

American Express, VISA/Barclaycard, MasterCard/Access, traveler's checks in pounds, U.S. dollars

Mail order

Skye Crotal Knitwear makes serious outdoors sweaters for men and women, traditional Fair Isles, and whimsical sweaters with rows of Scotties, sheep, rabbits, cats, clouds, or trees. The factory, once an abandoned school on the Sleat Peninsula of the Isle of Skye, has one of the finest views of any factory, and is one of few places where Gaelic is spoken daily. Crotal, from which the company takes its name, is a lichen found on the Isle of Skye that dyes yarns a lovely soft rust color.

People who wear larger sizes will find Skye Crotal a special bargain. Unlike the policy of many sweater factories, all sizes are one price, whether you are a 34-inch or a 46-inch size. There is a £2 charge for sizes over 46 inches or for knitting a sweater to specific measurements, which is quite reasonable for the extra work involved.

The Crofter, a medium-weight fisherman's rib in shetland or Harris yarns, is available in solid colors or with a double center stripe on chest and arms in sizes 34–46 inches. In a crewneck style (called a round neck), the sweater is £23.85; in a V-neck or polo-neck design (our turtleneck), it costs £24.85. It comes in 15 colors, but if your favorite color combination isn't available, your special order can be made in four to six weeks. The Islander is a heavier version of the Crofter, in solid shades of shetland yarn, available only as a crewneck. In shetland yarn, the sweater is £28.50. In the more expensive Harris yarn, the sweater costs £30.50. Used in the manufacture of Harris tweed, this yarn has a rough, hairy texture that makes it especially warm and durable.

Strath is a heavier version of the Islander that is knit in two alternating colors, giving the impression of a bird's-eye tweed. Available only as a crewneck, it costs £30.50 in shetland yarn and £32.50 in Harris.

The Fair Isle crewneck comes in small, medium, large, and extra large sizes and is especially pretty. It is a great value at £31 because the pattern is knitted all over the sweater, rather than only on the yoke, a more common and cheaper practice. The sweater comes in five color combinations, among them natural with moorit (a rich brown) and moss with natural.

All the picture sweaters—Scotties, sheep, rabbits,

cats, clouds, and trees—are shetland crewnecks, and all cost £32.85. They come in a variety of color combinations.

Best of all, there is a sale rack, where some sweaters are marked down 50 percent, from £24.85 to only £12.50, including some superb V-neck and turtleneck Crofter sweaters. There are a few seconds, too. A Scottie sweater was reduced from £32.50 to £23 because of a slight knitting flaw. The sale rack is a good area for bargain hunting.

Skye Silver
The Old School
Dunvegan
Isle of Skye N55 8GU
Tel. (047081) 263

Mon.–Sun. 10:00–6:00
Easter to end of September
American Express,
VISA/Barclaycard,
MasterCard/Access,
traveler's checks in pounds,
foreign currency
Mail order

Stewart Wilson's jewelry designs are inspired by three major sources: early Celtic art; the Jacobite rose, emblem of the Stuarts and especially of Bonnie Prince Charlie; and the Isle of Skye's seashore and famous Coral Beach at Loch Dunvegan.

Of the Celtic designs, made in vermeil (gold-plated sterling silver), four rings are especially pretty and would make unusual friendship rings or wedding bands: Borrodale (Celtic knotwork), Hamera (tree of life), Sunagill (forget-me-not), and Lorgill (cornucopia). Each is £22. Celtic scrolled-heart earrings are £13.80.

The Jacobite rose emblem looks best in sterling with a special white finish with polished highlights; some pieces are also available in 9-karat gold. The most attractive pieces are rose earrings for £14.50, a rose brooch for £39, and several pendants, ranging from £11.80 to £14.80.

Three seashore-motif pendants in sterling silver are very pretty with summer clothes: a whelk section for £19.50 (also available as a brooch at the same price), a chunk of driftwood for £65, and branch coral, availvailable in two sizes—one for £14.50 and one for £16.50.

Skye Venture Cottage Industry

18, Holmisdal
Glendale By Dunvegan
Isle of Skye IV43
Tel. (047081) 316

Mon.–Sat. 10:00–6:00
American Express,
*   VISA/Barclaycard,*
*   MasterCard/Access,*
*   traveler's checks in any*
*   currency*
Mail order

Skye Venture's Vargan sweater, knitted in fisherman's rib for warmth and resilience, with its natural oils retained, is the answer to the sailor's, hiker's, and climber's dreams. Owner W. A. Mackenzie offers words dear to a bargain hunter's heart: "We operate only one price structure—wholesale—so the tourist or visitor has the opportunity to purchase at the same price as the retailer or exporter."

The heavyweight ribbed oiled sweaters come in sizes 34–48 inches and in prices ranging from £26.95 to £31.95. They come in undyed natural shades of grays, browns, whites, and interesting combinations of grays or browns with white. Dyed colors offer more variety, with the prettiest shades a mid-blue, navy, and muted tweeds of green and gold or blue and lavender.

Handwoven tweeds from Skye Venture's own sheep are 30 inches wide and cost £6.50 per meter; hand-knitting yarns come in ten undyed shades, ranging from cream to black, for £21.60 per kilogram.

ORKNEY ISLES

Judith Glue   *Mon.–Sat. 9:30–5:30*
25 Broad Street   *VISA/Barclaycard,*
Kirkwall   *MasterCard/Access, U.S.*
Orkney Isles KW15 1DH   *dollars, traveler's checks in*
Tel. (0856) 4225   *pounds, personal checks*
                                     with ID
                                     Mail order, money orders in
                                     pounds

Many of Judith Glue's sweater designs reflect the historical Scandinavian influence on the culture of Orkney. Her pure wool knitwear comes in a wide range of patterns, styles, and colors suitable for men, women, and children. Hand-framed sweaters—made on hand-knitting machines—range from £22 to £45; hand-knitted sweaters are priced from £35 to £80. Sweaters come in all sizes: small (34–36 inches), medium (38–40 inches), and large (42–44 inches). Extra-large sizes are available by special order and for an additional cost of £3.

Judith Glue's selection is small, but uniformly beautiful, and most of her sweaters suit both men and women. Her Bright Carpet sweater, in bright blue, red, yellow, or green, costs £44.50. Her Tweedy Handknit sweater, which sells for £52, has a Fair Isle yoke and is available with a light gray background or a red-flecked black background. A Fair Isle sweater with browns and greens on a beige background costs £45 as a crewneck and £47.50 as a cardigan.

Orkney Rabbit has rows of charming black and white rabbits on a brown background. The crewneck, for men and women, is £45, and the ladies' cardigan is £49.50.

The most unusual group of sweaters in the collection is Judith Glue's Original Runic Knitwear. The pattern is taken from Viking runes (ancient graffiti?) found on the walls of the Maeshowe Neolithic chambered tomb. The design shows the word "Orkney" written in runic alphabet and is available as a men's leather-buttoned V-neck cardigan for £46.50, a ladies' wooden-buttoned crewneck cardigan at the same price, a sleeveless V-neck sweater for men and women for £33, and a crewneck for both for £43. Color combinations are subtle and beautiful: earth brown/green/blue, chestnut/blue/wine/green, black/gray/white, or amethyst/pink/gray.

Ola M. Gorie

Orkney Jewellery
The Longship
7/9 Broad Street
Kirkwall
Orkney Isles KW15 1DH
Tel. (0856) 3251

Mon.–Sat. 9:00–1:00,
2:00–5:30
VISA/Barclaycard,
MasterCard/Access,
traveler's checks in pounds
Mail order

Much of Ola Gorie's original silver and 9-karat gold jewelry shows strong Celtic and Norse influences. Some of her designs are based on the work of Charles Rennie Mackintosh, the famous Glasgow artist who gave art nouveau a special Scottish flavor, and some of her designs are derived from the Orkneys' local flowers and wildlife. Since I am prejudiced against 9-karat gold, often used in Britain, because it is only 37½ percent gold, with the rest base-metal alloy, I'll concentrate on Ola Gorie's lovely silver designs.

One of the nicest features of Ola Gorie's jewelry is its variety of sizes. A heart-shaped luckenbooth brooch—a traditional Scottish emblem also available as a pendant—comes in three sizes, costing £9, £15.05, and £25.60. A simpler luckenbooth design is used as a charm (£3.25) or as pierced or screwback earrings (£7.25).

Viking longships come as brooches for £9.60, £11.35, and £23.75, as pendants for £7.15, £9.50, and £22, as charms for £3.60 and £4.20, as pierced or screwback earrings for £8.00 and £9.50, and as cuff links for £18.85. The Viking galley also comes in a variety of sizes and jewelry items. Odin's Bird, an unusual design of a raven in a rhomboid frame, can be had as a brooch for £24.15, a pendant for £20.35, a charm for £3.30 or £3.70, pierced or screwback earrings for £3.30 or £7.50, or a ring for £7.70.

Designs derived from local Orkney archaeological sources are fascinating. The Maeshowe dragon looks as though it had stepped out of a medieval manuscript, and comes as a brooch for £11.15 and £25.30, a pendant for £8.60 and £23.35, a charm for £4, or pierced or screwback earrings for £9.10. Skara Brae, reminiscent of a primitive fleur-de-lis, is available as a brooch for £12.40, a pendant for £10.45, a charm for £3.90, pierced or screwback earrings for £8.70, and a ring for £7.80.

Many Celtic designs are based on the ninth-century *Book of Kells,* with interlacing motifs of lines, said to symbolize eternity, birds, animals, and man. Brooches are £15.45 and £20.90; pendants, some on silver chains, range from £12.40 to £20.70. Interlaced-pattern drop earrings sell for £9.50 and £9.80 in both pierced or screwback styles; two-headed bird earrings are £7.60.

Charles Rennie Mackintosh's influence is seen in two floral art nouveau designs, available as brooches for £19.55 and £27.40 and as pendants for £16.25 and £27.40. Another design, with strong, vertical lines, comes as a pendant attached to a chain for £19.10. Coordinating earrings are £12.90.

Flower motifs are used for stud and drop earrings, rings, pendants, and necklets (pendants attached to chains). Earrings range from £8.10 to £10.15 for drops and £6.45 to £7.25 for studs. Two especially pretty pendants are the fuchsia for £10 and the mistletoe for £13.70. Necklets range from £7.80 to £9.30, with a charming bluebell necklet selling for £9.

Ola Gorie also sells her discontinued designs and good-quality seconds ("most of the blemishes on the back only") at bargain prices. The discontinued spinning-wheel brooch, originally £14.10, was £7.60. The knight on horseback brooch, another discontinued design, was reduced from £24 to £13.95. As seconds, the Sjusta Brooch, a Norse pattern of intertwined animals and lines, was marked down from £21.50 to £13.70, and the Odin's Bird pendant, from £20.35 to £9.80.

Isle of Sanday Knitters (Orkney) Ltd.

Clairlea
Sanday
Orkney KW17 2BW
Tel. (08575) 380241 or
380340

By appointment
U.S. dollars and personal
checks with identification
Mail order

"Give us a ring any day, any time, and I will jump on my bicycle and be at the Wool Hall in Lady Village, in the center of the island, in ten minutes' time," says managing director Mrs. Elspeth Sinclair. She continues with words dear to a shopper's heart: "All our perfect stock is sold to visitors at wholesale price less 10 percent because we feel we must reward them for the effort in getting to our far-distant island."

With 43 colors in pure wool Icelandic Lopi yarns alone and with sizes from 20 to 46 inches, Isle of Sanday Knitters is a sweater lover's dream. Children's sweaters in bright random stripes are £4 for small (20–24 inches), £5 for medium (26–28 inches), and £6 for large (30–32 inches). (In adult sizes, they are only

£13.50.) Children's Lindsay sweaters—a lamb's wool crewneck with rabbit or other animal motif—is £7 for sizes 20–26 inches, £8.50 for sizes 28–30 inches, and only £5 as a slight second.

Children's hand-knitted Icelandic Lopi wool picture button-shoulder crewneck sweaters—a charming choice of snowman, apple tree, teddy bear, skier, baby geese (motifs in mohair), train, seagull, sheep, Scotties, Highland cattle, or fir trees—are £14 for small (22–24 inches), £16.50 for medium (26–28 inches), and £19.50 for large (30–32 inches). As slipover vests, they are £11 for small, £13.25 for medium, and £19.50 for large. Children's picture sweaters also come in thick cotton.

Children's sweaters are also available in traditional Icelandic crewnecks and cardigans and in lamb's wool with Fair Isle yokes. Matching hat, scarf, and mitten sets are £8.20.

Obviously, Isle of Sanday Knitters is a wonderful way to take care of the children on your Christmas and birthday lists, especially if you feel guilty about not having the time to knit beautiful presents yourself.

Now on to the more interesting adult sweaters. Hand-knitted Icelandic Lopi wool picture sweaters come in the children's patterns plus Christmas tree, bull, Mother Goose, a lighthouse, squares, triangles, and several other patterns. Crewneck sweaters are £28 for sizes 34–40 inches and £31 for sizes 42 and 44 inches. As slipover vests, they are £21 for sizes 34–40 inches and £23 for sizes 42 and 44 inches. If you'd like pictures on the back as well as the front, prices rise minutely: to £32 for crewneck sizes 34–42 inches and £25 for slipover sizes 34–42 inches.

Picture sweaters of your choice can be special-ordered. Mrs. Sinclair says, "Someone in Seattle wanted a moose, another person in Colorado wanted a cat, and so on. We do our own designs and are very adaptable."

Traditional Icelandic sweaters are a buy here, with most men's sweaters differing from women's only by size. Most sweaters are £26–£35. Cardigans range from £29.50 to £36, and vests (called waistcoats), from £22 to £27. All matching hats are £4.50; mittens are £5. Slight seconds in Icelandic sweaters go for bargain prices of £10–£20.

For dressier wear, women can put together a beautiful botany wool knit suit by combining a straight skirt for £12 with a classic cardigan for £12.50 (sizes 34–40 inches) or £14 (sizes 42 and 44 inches), the longer Elspeth cardigan with pockets for £19.75, or the lace-patterned Lucinda cardigan for £19.75. Under these: the Elspeth picot-edged sleeveless slipover for £9.75, the lace-patterned Lucinda sleeveless slipover for £12.30, or any classic crewneck or V-neck sweater for £9.50 (sizes 34–40 inches) or £11 (sizes 42–46 inches), or raglan-sleeved crewneck or V-neck sweater for £11 (sizes 34–40 inches) or £12.50 (sizes 42–46 inches). Total price: £34–£44.25, including VAT!

Or women can create a two-piece botany wool knit dress for around £30 by using the same skirt and any one of a dozen sweaters.

Be sure to check the sale rack. Current bargains: mohair sweaters that Isle of Sanday Knitters does exclusively for the posh boutique Browns of Bermuda are £30 if perfect and £20 as slight seconds. Batwing-sleeve mohair sweaters in pastels, combined with a V-shape insert in silky Italian yarn, are only £25.

Ortak Jewellery
Hatston Industrial Estate
Kirkwall, Orkney KW15
1RH
Tel. (0856) 2224

Mon.–Fri. 9:00–1:00,
2:00–5:00*
American Express, Diners
Club, VISA/Barclaycard,
MasterCard/Access
Mail order

*The shop at 10 Albert Street in Kirkwall is open Sat. 9:00–1:00 and 2:00–5:00

Ortak—from "Orkney" and the Norse for "thank you"—makes charming silver jewelry, including a large, lovely collection with local wildlife motifs, as well as the more common Scottish and Viking themes.

Among the wildlife pendants, the Scottish elk for £15.90, the deer for £11.50, the fox for £12.80, the puffin for £17.50, the woodpecker for £13.20, and the heron, also for £13.20, are especially attractive. Collectors of charms will find a great variety of wildlife and other charms ranging from £2.60 to £15, with most of them in the £4 to £6 range. Wildlife motifs are also featured on brooches, mostly within circular frames. An owl is £17, a swan £16.60, a puffin £18.70, and an osprey £18.20. Two otters playing on a log are £15.20. Among the brooches that have no frame, a small Shetland pony costs £13.90, but the brooch made by Shetland Silvercraft (see p. 242) is larger, more detailed, and a far better buy at £19.75—only about $8.50 more. Better detail is found on the deer brooch for £10.60 and the little fox brooch for £9.

Ortak has an excellent collection of decorative demitasse spoons (called coffee spoons) and teaspoons. The demitasse spoons range from £17.20 for a spoon with an owl in a circular frame as the handle to £20.30 for a spoon with the Maeshowe dragon (see below) as the handle. A £19.50 spoon with a thistle as the handle is very pretty and resembles a pineapple, the traditional symbol of hospitality. Teaspoons range from £18.10 for the owl-handled spoon to £21.20 for the spoon with the Maeshowe dragon. The thistle-handled spoon costs £20.70; there is also an interesting spoon with a bezel-set onyx as the handle for £21.

Men's plain silver cuff links are very reasonable. Small ovals cost £15.30, and larger ones, £18.80. These two models have chain fittings. Cut-corner rectangles cost £19.30 and have swivel fittings, as do the oval cuff links with a lion rampant, the heraldic symbol of Scotland, for £25.50.

Ortak's scallop-shell earrings, priced at £11.20, are quite attractive. The earrings set with semiprecious stones carry more punch than most of the plain silver earrings. My favorites are the carnelians bezel-set in silver for £10.80 and £13.80 and the tigereye drops bezel-set in silver for £14.30.

Among Ortak's Scottish designs, the Scottish terrier brooch for £14.50 and the lion rampant for £14.10 are the most charming and would add zip to a hat—especially a beret—as well as to a jacket or sweater. Penannular (ring-shaped) brooches are more traditional: two modern-design brooches are £21.10 and £23.80; more Celtic-looking brooches with engraved strapwork cost £23.50, £31.90, and £37.60. Some Celtic brooches that feature knotwork interlacing cost £18, £30.10, and £31.60—the last in an interesting octagonal design. Of all of Ortak's luckenbooth jewelry (heart motifs, usually intertwined—a symbol of love and betrothal in Scotland since the 17th century), my clear favorite is an ultrasimple version with wirework highlights that could have been made by Georg Jensen. It costs £14.80.

Skara Brae, resembling a primitive version of the fleur-de-lis, comes from one of the best preserved prehistoric villages in Europe, discovered in Orkney. The motif appears on pendants, earrings, bracelets, rings, and cuff links, but I don't think it is as appealing as the Maeshowe dragon, which was carved by Norse raiders on the wall of a Neolithic burial chamber discovered in the Orkney Islands.

The Maeshowe dragon looks best in big pieces because its details are clearest. The large brooch is £23.70. The largest pendant is £15, and the largest earrings, £7.20. The £24 bracelet of nine linked motifs is interesting because the delicacy of the bracelet plays against the ferocity of the beast.

Ortak also has a wide selection of kilt pins and thistle-motif jewelry.

People who buy a lot will receive a discount based on the size of their order. Ortak discounts discontinued designs 25–35 percent, but there is no knowing whether such pieces will be available whenever you visit.

Look for sales in January.

Shetland Isles

Reawick (Shetland) Lamb Marketing Company Ltd

Skeld
Reawick
Shetland ZE2 9NJ
Tel. (059586) 261

Mon.–Fri. 8:00–5:00
Traveler's checks in pounds,
  personal checks with ID
Mail order by inquiry

Reawick's sheepskin products and garments are a by-product of the company's abattoir, where only 4,000–5,000 of the best sheepskins and lambskins are chosen every season.

Sheepskins and sheepskin rugs come in all sizes, colors, and shapes. "A" grade white sheepskins are £16, "B" grade £15.50, and "C" grade £12.50. "A" grade white lambskins, which are smaller and finer than sheepskins, are £13.50, "B" grade £13, and "C" grade £11.50. Natural-colored sheepskins start at £15.50, depending on the rarity of the pattern. Double-size white rugs are £25.50 (small), £29 (medium), and £36 (large); patterned rugs vary between £27.75 and £34.50. Twin-size bedspreads range from £92 to £97.75; double, queen-size, and king-size bedspreads have to be special-ordered.

Children's sheepskin clothing stands out here, and there is no VAT on it. Vests come in small, medium, and large sizes, fleece side in or out, for £11.30–£15.90.

Dyed vests are £12.80–£17.70, and a set consisting of matching dyed vest, hat, and muff is £21.50–£26.65. Bought separately, the hat is £5.65 and the muff is £4.60.

Women's vests are £19.44–£23.98 for a style with the fleece side out, £23.58–£27.14 for a style with the fleece side in, and £26.68–£29.73 for dyed vests. Hats are £8.97, ski hats are £11.50, and slippers are £6.90.

Shetland Silvercraft	*Mon.–Fri. 8:00–1:00,*
Soundside	*2:00–5:00*
Weisdale	*American Express,*
Shetland ZE2 9BR	*VISA/Barclaycard,*
Tel. (059572) 275	*MasterCard/Access,*
	traveler's checks in pounds,
	foreign currency
	Mail order

Shetland Silvercraft has made beautiful silver jewelry for over thirty years, its designs inspired by Norse mythology, by archaeological finds discovered in the Shetlands, and by local wildlife.

Shetland Silvercraft's jewelry is larger, heavier, more detailed and more expensive than that made by its competitors, but it is well worth the difference in price. A large Shetland pony brooch has a mane and tail so clearly defined that you can count the individual hairs; it costs £19.75. A Shetland collie brooch, with equally fine detail, also costs £19.75. A brooch of the Shetland wren within a rounded rectangular silver frame is £24.50, and a brooch of an osprey within a stylized wide triangular frame is £19.95. An unusual brooch of a fish rising through ripples sells for only £14.95. A kilt pin in a ram's head design looks simultaneously archaic and supermodern. A welcome change from all those sword-and-thistle kilt pins, it costs £27.75. Even the thistle brooches take on a new look here, with two asymmetric designs selling for only £11.75 and £15.80, and a thistle brooch bordered in a geometric motif reminiscent of the designs of Charles Rennie Mackintosh, Scotland's greatest arts-and-crafts movement designer, for £14.50.

Among the jewelry inspired by Norse mythology, brooches depicting the three Norns (Fates) in their guise as swans, and Odin, chief of the Norse gods, riding Sleipnir, his eight-legged steed, are the most fascinating. The swan brooch—about 3 inches long—costs £28.95. The Sleipnir brooch comes in three sizes, priced at £13.35, £17.75, and £29.50.

Of the archaeologically inspired pieces, two brooches stand out. The Anglian Beast is a large zoomorphic design whose head and general silhouette resemble a horse—until the tail, which weaves all around the beast. It's a knockout for £38.50. The Quendale Beast is a reproduction of a bronze harness ornament found on the beach at Quendale. Since part of this griffinlike ornament was missing, owner/designer Jack Rae designed the beast's head to fit in with the original artifact. The brooch comes in three sizes, priced at £12.30, £17.50, and £29.50.

One Viking ship brooch is quite unusual because it reduces the ship to a line drawing, made of silver wire; it costs £16.75. Other Viking ship brooches are available, but this one and a large well-modeled piece discontinued recently and therefore marked down from £25 to £21 are the stars of this collection.

Earrings for pierced and unpierced ears are available, but their size and price (£5.95–£12.50) preclude a great deal of detail. The most interesting are the Quendale Beast and Sleipnir for £8.95 each, the Anglian Beast for £12.50, and squarish studs, for £9.95, depicting a detail from a hoard of silver discovered on St. Ninian Isle in the Shetlands in 1958.

Shetland Silvercraft also makes some attractive silver jewelry for men. The Quendale Beast tie tack is

£11.95; matching cuff links are £19.50. The Sleipnir tie tack is £11.95; matching cuff links are £21. All cuff links are available with either chain or swivel fittings.

WESTERN ISLES

Hebridean Jewellery
Garrieganichy
Iochdar
South Uist, Western Isles
   PA81 5QX
Tel. (08704) 288

Mon.–Sat. 9:00–5:00
VISA/Barclaycard,
   MasterCard/Access,
   traveler's checks in pounds
Mail order

Hebridean Jewellery is a manufacturer of traditional Celtic jewelry in sterling silver and 9-karat gold. Admittedly, I am prejudiced against 9-karat gold, which is only 37½ percent gold, with the rest base-metal alloy, so I'll concentrate on Hebridean Jewellery's beautiful silver designs.

Kilt pins are quite attractive. Two, in the shape of swords, are £15 and £20. A smaller thistle shape is £16. Most interesting of the group are an unusual braided shape for £26.60 and an animal-headed, interlaced design for £30.40, both typically Celtic.

Luckenbooth brooches are very popular. A traditional Scottish emblem, the luckenbooth is heart-shaped, frequently two intertwined hearts surmounted by a crown. Luckenbooth brooches have been popular as lovers' gifts since the late 17th century. Hebridean has numerous designs, including one that is almost abstract in form for £17, a simple one of two intertwined scrolling hearts for £16, and an old-fashioned one with a chased pattern for £17.

Penannular brooches (open circles pierced with stickpins) have been used for over 2,000 years—originally to fasten cloaks and tunics—and are Hebridean's most popular piece of jewelry. Brooch designs make use of Celtic interlacing motifs, said to symbolize eternity. Prices are £19 and £25.80. Other interesting brooches are the Scottish heraldic lion rampant, supporting the Scottish flag emblazoned with the cross of St. Andrew, for £14; a fish that must come right out of a medieval manuscript for £17; and a snake superimposed on a line turning up at one end, down at the other, for £19. The design for that unusual brooch came from a Pictish stone carving in Perthshire.

Charms, which are of thistle, luckenbooth, Scottish lion, or Celtic interweave design, can also be worn as pendants or ordered as earrings, cuff links, tie tacks, or bracelets. Earrings, which range in price from £8.30 to £11 for pierced postback closures, can be ordered with screwbacks or clips for unpierced ears, or with drop-wire fittings for pierced ears for an additional 80p. The prettiest designs are modern and traditional thistles, a small, tailored-looking luckenbooth, and clan crests.

Hebridean's silver rings are very attractive. The Scottish lion is £10.20 or £17, depending on the weight. Similarly, thistle rings are £11.40 and £17. Luckenbooth rings sell for £10.20 and £11.40. Unusual Celtic interlaced animals cost £11.40. Women's clan crest rings are priced at £17, and men's, at £19.

Chapter 14 *The Rest of Scotland*

EXEXEXE

This, too, is a portmanteau chapter that includes wonderful factory outlets and crafts shops scattered all over Scotland. Although they're spread out all over the country, they're well worth a visit if you are anywhere nearby—and you may see some beautiful countryside and find a charming little pub or inn while you're getting there.

ALVA

Inverallan Hand Knitters Limited
Shavelhaugh Loan
Alva
Clackmannanshire FK12 5DQ
Tel. (0259) 62292

By appointment
Traveler's checks in pounds, foreign currency
Mail order

Inverallan is the largest hand-knitting company in Europe: its 2,500 knitters produce over 25,000 sweaters per year. Since Ireland is Inverallan's largest market, it makes sense to buy here and avoid the middleman.

Inverallan permits foreign tourists to buy direct from them at wholesale prices in one of two ways: either by buying from the overrun box, which always contains at least 50 or 60 sweaters, or by ordering a sweater in their size and color. These sweaters take about six weeks to make.

The permutations and combinations of design, color, type of yarn, and even choice of buttons are staggering. Choose from four crewneck patterns, five cardigan patterns, and three vest patterns, Aran yarn (natural plus 23 colors), Donegal tweed (12 colors), Donegal fleck (10 colors), a 50 percent cotton/50 percent wool blend (16 colors), 8-ply cotton (20 colors), 9-ply lamb's wool (14 colors), or even 9-ply cashmere.

Prices for a crewneck in Aran yarn range from £25 for a woman's size 34 inches to £40 for a man's size 46 inches. In 9-ply lamb's wool, the prices range from £34 to £57. Prices for the same sweater in cashmere are between £110 and £200, depending on the color chosen, with light shades being the most expensive. Even at £200 less the VAT (roughly $250–$275), they are a great bargain; in New York those sweaters sold for over $1,000 in 1986.

Children's sweaters are not stock items, but can be made to order.

CRIEFF

Stuart Strathearn Limited

Muthill Road
Crieff
Perthshire PH7 4HQ
Tel. (0764) 4004

Mon.–Sat. 9:00–5:00, Sun. 11:00–5:00
American Express, Diners Club, VISA/Barclaycard, MasterCard/Access, traveler's checks in pounds Mail order—inquire first

Stuart Strathearn's factory shop sells items from Stuart Crystal, its parent company in Stourbridge in the English Midlands (see p. 105 for a full description of stemware and accessories), as well as its own Strathearn

Collection's sand-engraved crystal and colored crystal giftware. Slight seconds sell for approximately one-third less than the retail price, and discontinued first-quality pieces sell for half their original price, including VAT, so your net price works out to half or less of British retail prices and much less than half of U.S. retail prices.

The Strathearn Collection uses traditional Scottish motifs. Elegance, a 9½-inch oval vase engraved with a poppy or morning glory, is £19.75. Wildwood, a 6-inch oval vase engraved with a dog rose, thistle, honeysuckle, or daffodil, costs £10. Teardrop, a 5-inch oval vase engraved with a snowdrop, rose, thistle, bluebell, fuchsia, daffodil, or primrose, is only £5.70. Mystique, a 7¼-inch bud vase engraved with a rose, field mouse, bird, bluebell, foxglove, or poppy, sells for £6, while Romance, a 5½-inch bud vase engraved with a butterfly, rose, pansy, or thistle, sells for £5.35.

Morning Dew Rose bowls, each engraved with a rose, thistle, or honeysuckle, are £5 for the miniature size, £6.35 for the 2½-inch size, and £11 for the 4-inch size. Spirit of the Glens decanters, priced at £23.50, are engraved with a stag, leaping salmon, osprey, or pheasant, and matching 8-ounce rummers (similar to old-fashioned glasses) are £4.65 each. Thistle-engraved Scottish Mist decanters are also £23.50, while matching 5-ounce rummers are £4.

Strathearn's Colored Crystal collection is magnificent. Ebony & Gold starts with hand-blown black crystal in contemporary shapes, each rolled in 23-karat gold to create abstract patterns of pure gold against gleaming black. Very Japanese, very elegant. Ginger jars (called urn vases), perfect for flowers or as lamps, come in four sizes: the 9½-inch size is £33.50; the 8½-inch, £25, the 6½-inch, £16.75; and the 5½-inch, £11.00. Elliptical vases come in five sizes: the 12-inch size is £33.50; the 9-inch, £25; the 6½-inch, £16.75; the 5-inch, £10; and the 3½-inch, £6.70. There are also oblong and cylindrical vases in 11-, 9-, 7½-, 5½-, and 4-inch heights. Bowls come in three sizes: the 10-inch size is £33.50; the 8-inch, £20; and the 6-inch, £13.25.

Witch bowls are a fascinating term and shape that may be unfamiliar to American readers. Centuries ago, when people feared witchcraft, they would place candles in bowls whose wide shoulders and tapered necks protected the flame from drafts. They hung these lighted bowls in their windows at night to keep away evil spirits. The old superstition is gone, and witch bowls now make pretty containers for short-stemmed flowers. They are available in 9-inch (£28.50), 7-inch (£16.75), 5½- (£11.75), and 4-inch (£8.70) sizes.

Strathearn's Dark Crystal Collection blends hand-blown black crystal with soft-colored red or white glass powders to produce subtle textures and colors. Prices are approximately 20 percent lower than those of identical Ebony & Gold pieces. The Impressions Collection —white glass with pink or green impressionistic patterns—is the same price as the Dark Crystal Collection.

ELGIN

The Mill Shop   *Mon.–Sat. 9:00–5:30*
Newmill   *VISA/Barclaycard,*
Elgin IV30 2AF   *MasterCard/Access*
Tel. (0343) 7821   *Mail order*

The Mill Shop is the outlet of Johnstons of Elgin and carries knitwear in cashmere, wool, and shetland, fabrics, yarn, kilts, skirts, jackets, ties, scarves, rugs, and a variety of Scottish crafts and souvenirs. Cashmere prices have risen 20–25 percent since 1985, but they're still a good buy, with ladies' doubleweight (2-ply) pullovers for £39.50 and men's doubleweight V-neck sweaters for £39.50. Hand-knitted Aran sweaters for men and women are a great buy at £30.50—

oddly enough, less expensive than they are in much of Ireland—as are women's wool kilted skirts in tartans, navy, or gray for £22.50. Children's kilted skirts run from £8.20 to £13.40, depending on the length and size. Plaid cashmere scarves in tartans and solids for £19.75 make excellent presents, as do cashmere gloves for £6.95 and £8 and the 70 percent cashmere/30 percent wool lightweight blanket for £37.75.

FALKIRK

MacIntosh Glass
Dalderse Avenue
Falkirk FK2 7EG
Tel. (0324) 37986

Mon.–Fri. 9:00–12:00,
1:00–5:00; also by
appointment
Traveler's checks in pounds
Mail order—inquire first

MacIntosh Glass makes perfume bottles, bowls, paperweights, and vases, many of them with multicolor swirls and ribbons. Slight seconds are usually available for just a little over wholesale prices—an extremely good value—making it well worth the 40-mile westward drive from Edinburgh.

Vertex, a vertical-striped pattern in red, blue, green, or yellow, is available in a miniature perfume bottle for £8.60, a small perfume bottle for £8.70, a heavy-bottomed perfume bottle for £15, and a paperweight for £6.50.

Helix is a swirled pattern of red/amethyst, red/blue, blue/green, red/amethyst/blue, yellow/green/blue, red/yellow/amethyst, and white opal. Perfume bottles cost £8.60–£12 in the bicolor combinations and £9.50–£12.50 in the tricolor combinations and in white opal. Miniature bowls are £4.60 in bicolor and £5.20 in tricolor and white opal; 4-inch dishes are £5.30 in bicolor and £6 in tricolor and white opal.

Vases are available in Wynd, a pattern with a horizontal blue swirl. Both the tall and round bases are £20. Bowls and plates are available in Carron, with blue or amethyst diagonal lines. Bowls are £13, miniature bowls £4.25, plates £15, and 4-inch dishes £5.50.

Leny, a pattern with coppery-blue bubbles, is one of MacIntosh's most interesting patterns. Small perfume bottles are priced at £12, and large ones, at £14.50, while small paperweights cost £7.20, and large ones, £14.50.

KIRKCUDBRIGHT AND KIRKCUDBRIGHTSHIRE

David Gulland
Engraved Glass
Skairkilndale
Kirkcudbright
Galloway DG6 4BG
Tel. (0557) 31072

Mon.–Fri. 2:00–5:30
VISA/Barclaycard, traveler's
checks in pounds
Mail order

David Gulland makes beautiful engraved glass and crystal, whose most elaborate designs compare favorably with those of Steuben Crystal. Items and prices vary greatly—no surprise, as most of his work consists of one-of-a-kind commissioned pieces. A small glass posy vase with a simple sandblasted design of a wildflower is £8; the same design done as a more elaborate, time-consuming copper-wheel engraving on a 24-percent lead crystal vase costs £25. A more complicated design—a wild animal or bird—on a set of six glasses is £50; a copper-wheel-engraved version on crystal would cost £200.

Among Gulland's more beautiful pieces are a bowl engraved with two playful otters chasing fish (£250), a paperweight engraved with an otter (£50), a vase engraved with a dragon (£100), a perfume bottle engraved with lilies of the valley (£60), and one engraved with rock-garden plants (£70).

Commissioned pieces take six to twelve weeks; simpler monograms and logos can usually be done within three weeks.

Anne Hughes Pottery
Auchreoch
Balmaclellan
Kirkcudbrightshire DG7 3QB
Tel. (06442) 205

Mon.–Sat. 10:00–6:00
May–Sept.; also by
appointment
Cash only

You may remember reading briefly about Anne Hughes's striking pierced pottery in the section about Edinburgh's Scottish Craft Centre (p. 125). If you like her work, you may wish to drive to her studio, about 75 miles southwest of Edinburgh, and buy directly from her.

Anne Hughes makes hand-thrown domestic stoneware and individual pierced bowls, plates, and jars in ice blue, lichen green, honey, and coffee. Prices at her studio range from £2 for a simple necklace to £40 for some of her more intricate pierced plates, in comparison to £55–£60 at the Scottish Craft Centre and over £80 in retail shops.

Items include mugs, casseroles, vases, and plant bowls with pierced rims. One of her best buys is a cruet set consisting of salt and pepper shakers, salad-dressing bottle, and mustard pot with its own little spoon, all on a matching plate; the cost for the entire set is only £13.20. Probably the artist's most popular small piece is her posy pot, a round, beautifully decorated pierced vase, for only £3.90.

LANGHOLM

Devra King

Nethernock
Bentpath
Langholm
Dumfriesshire DG13 0PB
Tel. (05413) 288

By appointment
Traveler's checks in
pounds

Devra King's large, bulky 3- and 4-ply hand-knitted cashmere sweaters use updated cable and other traditional knitting stitches and big-shouldered modern silhouettes. Her customers include Neiman-Marcus, Bergdorf Goodman, Henri Bendel, and San Francisco's Cashmeres of Scotland, and Scotch House in London. U.S. retail prices for her sweaters are around $500–$600.

Devra always has sample sweaters and overstocks in bright jewel colors, pastels, and neutrals at her studio, and they'll cost only £125–£155 after the VAT has been refunded. Sometimes she also has matching or coordinating skirts, which cost only £90 after the VAT refund.

PERTH

Caithness Glass PLC

Inveralmond
Perth PH1 3EE
Tel. (0738) 37373

Mon.–Sat. 9:00–5:00, Sun.
1:00–5:00; Sun. in
July–Aug. 11:00–5:00
American Express, Diners
Club, VISA/Barclaycard,
MasterCard/Access,
traveler's checks in
pounds

Caithness Glass is probably best known for its crystal paperweights, but the company also makes very attractive engraved glass, including floral, wildlife, and sports motifs; a collection of tableware in peat, heather, and clear glass; Stroma, a collection of bowls and vases in heather, moss green, peat, and amethyst glass; Cadenza, a collection of vases in opalescent peacock blue; Spinningdale, a collection of vases and bowls in which delicate threads of multicolor glass are spun into the clear, heather, or moss green body of the piece; and Rondo, a collection of vases in six shapes with swirls of rose, azure, sable, or emerald glass throughout.

In addition to first-quality items, sold at full retail prices, the factory shop stocks a full range of slight seconds in glassware, engraved glass, paperweights (unlimited editions only), and jewelry. Prices range from £3.95 to £50, and discounts from retail prices range from 40 percent to a high of 80 percent. The posy vases in Rondo, which are £6.95 if perfect, are £3.95 here, and the beautiful large bowl in Stroma, which sells for £16.50 if perfect, is only £4.95 here. Unlimited-edition paperweights, which are £8.95 to £136 if perfect, sell for £4.95 to £25 as slight seconds. Caithness's large Perth factory outlet and its sister shops in Wick (see p. 153) and Oban (see p. 151) are well worth visiting.

Highland Character Dolls

Fechney
Spens Crescent
Perth PH1 1PE
Tel. (0738) 34956

By appointment
Traveler's checks in pounds,
*   personal checks with ID*
Mail order

Sheena Macleod's Highland Character Dolls are signed pieces, prized especially by American, Canadian, Australian, and Japanese collectors. Prices at her workshop in Perth are about the same as retail prices "because production is limited and there are no seconds or rejects—these are broken down." The advantage of buying directly from the creator is that Ms. Macleod autographs figures bought from her personally, whereas her dolls that are bought elsewhere are not signed.

The most popular character doll is a little old woman at her spinning wheel. It comes in a display box and costs £32.50–£34.50. Another popular figure is a fisherman making a wooden creed and sells for about the same price. Prices for dolls sent airmail to the United States are the same as those bought in Scotland because the VAT is about the same as the cost of postage.

St. Andrews

Largo Pottery *Mon.–Sat. 10:00–5:00*
Church Square Ceramics *Apr.–Dec.*
St. Andrews, Fife KY16 *Traveler's checks in pounds*
9NN
Tel. (0334) 77744

Anne Lightwood's Largo Pottery porcelain is handmade, assembled carefully from many segments of colored clay placed together like a mosaic, then rolled and pressed over a mold. In this way, the pattern and color are an integral part of the piece, and no two pieces are ever identical, although many harmonize enough to make up a set of four or more. Instead of glaze, Anne Lightwood seals each piece with beeswax to create a burnished surface similar to that of a polished pebble.

For an artisan whose work is in the Royal Scottish

Museum in Edinburgh and in many private collections in Britain and the United States, Anne Lightwood's one-of-a-kind pieces seem amazingly inexpensive, with most priced between £3 and £40. Best buys are her small shell-like dishes selling between £3 and £7, and her vases with landscape, wave, or rainbow motifs priced from £7 to £9.

SKIRLING

Douglas Davies Pottery
Loanfoot
Skirling
Biggar
Lanarkshire ML12 6HD
Tel. (08996) 254

Mon.–Sat. 9:00–6:00; also by appointment
Traveler's checks in pounds, foreign currency
Mail order

Douglas Davies's rough, ribbony ceramics have been exhibited at the Edinburgh Festival, both in Edinburgh and in Osaka, Japan, at the Salzburg Festival in Linz, Austria, at the International Art Fair in London, and at many one-man shows in Edinburgh. In addition, he has made commissioned pieces for the Theatre Royal of Glasgow and the president of Austria. His works are in the Royal Scottish Museum.

Yet, despite these impressive credentials, Davies's work is surprisingly affordable. Mugs are only £2; pitchers, £2, £3, £4, and £10, depending on the size; cheese dishes and casseroles, £10–£20; hanging plant pots, £4–£20; and porcelain bottles, £15–£30. Attractive white crackle-glazed vases with the rough-ribboned handles that are Davies's trademark are £25 for the 7-inch size and £30 for the 10-inch size.

Davies's larger pieces are more expensive. Large one-of-a-kind black ceramic planters, similar to the ones he made for Glasgow's City Chamber, are 36 inches high and cost £150–£200. A 15-inch reduced-stoneware landscape-motif platter with a dry-glazed center and an unglazed stony rim is £50. Other decorative one-of-a-kind pieces—often massive and strong in form and color—range from £50 to £175.

Part Four

Wales

Chapter 15 *Wales: The Basics*

Wales is a magical land. Its praises sung by poets and bards, its hundreds of beautifully preserved castles, excite the imagination and invite the visitor. Its towering mountains, sweeping national parks, and miles of beaches make Wales a nature lover's paradise.

Wales is a shopper's paradise, too. Welsh wool is famed throughout the British Isles; Welsh pottery is well known, too. As you might expect, prices are much lower in Wales than in London or in any other large British cities. Driving is the best way to get around and will give you the opportunity to experience the magnificent Welsh countryside.

While most people think of Wales as being hundreds of miles from London, Cardiff, the Welsh capital and a good jumping-off point for traveling through Wales, is only 1¾ hours away on British Rail's high-speed InterCity 125 trains, which, as their name implies, reach speeds of 125 miles per hour. If you take the early-morning train, you'll get into Cardiff around 10:00, with a full day ahead of you to begin exploring Wales.

What to Buy

Sweaters and fabrics made of Welsh wool, wool clothing, yarns, blankets and quilts, pottery, pewter, and jewelry—some even made with gold mined in

Wales. Remember to bring ample cash and traveler's checks; most Welsh factory outlets and crafts shops do not take credit cards.

1986 CURRENCY RANGE

Wales is part of Britain and uses the British pound. See p. 27 for currency range.

THE VAT

See p. 29.

GETTING IT BACK

See p. 29.

TELEPHONE NUMBERS

See p. 29.

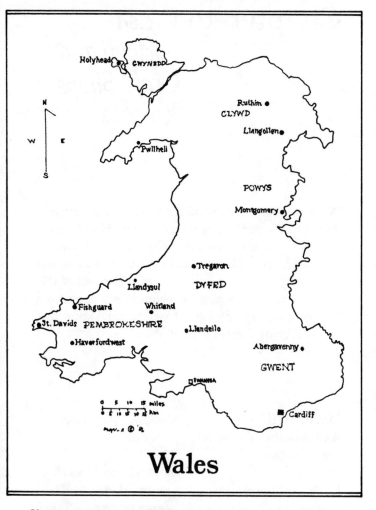

Wales

Shopping sources in Wales are spread out, but well worth traveling to. Welsh factory and crafts shops offer some of the most beautiful and unusual gifts in the British Isles.

Chapter 16 *Welsh Factory and Craft Shops*

Wales has many more small crafts workers and artisans than it has factories. The places written about here are located in six major counties: Clwyd, Dyfed, Gwent, Gwynedd, Pembrokeshire, and Powys. They are spread out, but that's part of the charm of Wales and of this kind of shopping: seeing the country as you go from factory to factory, workshop to workshop. I know that you will enjoy the beauties of Wales.

CLWYD

Jakim Artifacts
Sundials and Art Casting by
*   Andrew Evans*
Unit 4
Ruthin Craft Centre
Ruthin
Clwyd LL15 1BP
Tel. (08242) 5414

Mon.–Sun. 10:00–6:00;
*   closed Dec. 25–26 and*
*   Jan. 1*
Traveler's checks in pounds,
*   personal checks with ID,*
*   foreign currency*
Mail order

Andrew Evans designs some of the world's greatest and most original range of sundials, which can even be personalized. He also makes marvelous sculptures that can adorn the sundials or be used on their own.

Each sundial is handmade and can be constructed for any latitude in the world. The standard United Kingdom sundials are set for latitude 55° N. New Yorkers would need latitude 40°30′ N; Washingtonians, latitude 39° N; Floridians, latitudes 31°–25° N, depending on location; and Californians, latitudes 42°–32°30′ N, depending on location.

Most sundials are designed to be mounted horizontally; a good number can also be mounted on walls that face south, southwest or southeast, south-southwest, south-southeast, west-southwest, and east-southeast. One can even be mounted on a wall facing either east or west.

Flat sundials range from £18 to £57.50; statuary sundials run as high as £130. Nameplates can add an additional £30 to the cost. Among my favorites: an octagonal sundial with a beaming sun for £38.50, a crescent-shaped sundial with two lions' heads for £48.50, a rectangular sundial with a cherub and scrolls in the corners for £48.50, and an ornate-shaped one with a cupid for £65.

The statuary sundials—Rhocos, Icarus, and the Sundial Bearer—would grace any garden, as would the 11- to 15-inch bronze figurative sculptures entitled Dancer, Standing Figure, Bronze Ring, and Leaping Figure—each in editions of 25—for £150–£190.

Dermot and Lynda Kay
Potters
Pontrefelin Mill
Llangollen
Clwyd LL20 8EE
Tel. (0978) 860602

Mon.–Sun. early July–mid-Sept. and most of the year, but telephone first
Traveler's checks in pounds

Dermot and Lynda Kay specialize in stoneware pottery for indoors and outdoors. Their outdoor pieces are frostproof—ideal for American gardens—and their kitchenware goes from freezer to oven or microwave to dishwasher.

Their price range is quite wide, but there is a large selection in the £5 to £15 range, including a collection of tiny bottles, jars, and bowls in a variety of colors that can be tucked into odd corners of your suitcase.

Among the Kays' larger pieces, the "vine" goblet is especially attractive. It is a larger version of a wine goblet, in 10 and 14-inch sizes. You can plant directly in it or put a flowerpot inside, to create height in an indoor or outdoor display of plants. The 10-inch size costs £10, and the 14-inch size, £30.

A bread crock is another favorite. It keeps bread fresh and moist without the risk of its becoming moldy, even in the hottest weather. The large size is £25, and the smaller size, £15. The most popular color is a bright toasty brown, just the shade of a fresh-baked, crusty loaf.

Dyfed

Brambles
Blaengwrfach Ufach
Bancyffordd
Llandysul
Dyfed SA44 4RY
Tel. (055932) 2665

"Any reasonable time"
Mar.–Sept.; call for
appointment
Traveler's checks in pounds,
personal checks with ID
Mail order

"Brambles" is the English word for "blackberries," an evocative name for this beautiful country location where Sue Watkins makes lovely handmade patchwork items using traditional patterns and modern materials. She is a member of the Quilter's Guild and specializes in nursery quilts, double-size quilts, and cushions in the Log Cabin, Hexagon Wheel, Dresden Plate, and Folded Star patterns, and in dressing-table or needlework baskets in Folded Star. She also makes bags, pincushions, place mats, tea cozies, children's clothing, and many other items, and will take commission orders.

Prices range from £1 for a patchwork pincushion to £200 for quilts to fit a double bed.

Canolfan Cynllun Crefft Cymru
Craft Design Centre of Wales
Main Square
Tregaron
Dyfed SY25 6JL
Tel. (09744) 415

Mon.–Sat. 9:00–5:30
year-round; Sun.
10:00–6:00
mid-June–mid-Sept.
VISA/Barclaycard,
MasterCard/Access,
traveler's checks in pounds,
foreign currency
Mail order

The Craft Design Centre of Wales is the best craft outlet in Wales. Rhiannon Jewellery is made here, as is Brethyn Cartref, ethnic knitwear in natural-colored undyed wools.

Rhiannon—Jewellery in the Celtic medium—is designed and made by Rhiannon S. Evans, the silversmith who also runs the Craft Design Centre. Her Celtic art forms are not copies of museum pieces but original creations, inspired by ancient Welsh legends, from a period when Britain and Ireland were regarded as a single country. The legendary Rhiannon is one such character, who came from the magical Otherworld of Annwn ("That Without Depth") to live among the mortals of Dyfed. Magical cycles of exchanged identity play a part in these legends, thus the mirror imagery of many of Rhiannon's designs.

Although Rhiannon's designs are available in sterling silver, 9-karat gold, and 18-karat gold, I find they offer the best value in silver, where they are priced from £7 to £50. Similar pieces in 9-karat gold, which is only 37½ percent gold, with the rest base-metal alloy, range from £30 to £300. The same items in 18-karat gold vary between £70 and £500, but sometimes there might be samples, one-of-a-kind pieces, and discontinued items in 18-karat gold that would be bargain-priced.

One of Rhiannon's most dramatic pieces is the Gelert brooch, modeled after a Celtic cloak pin. It is a heavy three-dimensional piece representing an Irish wolfhound—perhaps the Gelert of Welsh legend—and costs £49.50. Cwn Annwn (The Hounds of Annwn) is an intricate knotwork pendant attached to a 16-inch heavy rope chain, with hand-engraved surface detail, and costs £44. Ceir Cwm Cych (The Deer of Cwm Cych) is a design derived from the legend of Pwyll, the prince of Dyfed, and Rhiannon in the *Mabinogion,* the Welsh national epic poem. The deer motif, based on a single deer carved on a stone cross in Scotland, has been duplicated in a mirror-image design. The piece, available as a pendant on a fine 16-inch chain or as a brooch, costs £18.95. March Rhiannon (Rhiannon's Horse) is derived from the famous White Horse of Uffington, an early Celtic carving on a chalk hillside in southern England that measures almost 100 meters. In legend, Rhiannon is associated with the horse. As a brooch or a pendant on a 16-inch rope chain, the piece costs £25.50; a smaller version on a finer chain costs £13.50.

The smaller Celtic knot design is attractive as pierced earrings (£20.50), as screwback earrings or cuff links (£22.50), as a stickpin (£11.50), or as a pendant on an 18-inch fine chain (£13.50). Celtic hoop earrings for pierced ears are pretty and delicate and cost only £10.

Jewelry seconds, with only minuscule flaws, offer exceptional values and are often discounted 50 percent —to the cost of the precious metal itself.

Brethyn Cartref Knitwear makes traditional woolen sweaters, hats, and scarves for men, women, and children—most hand-framed (made on hand-knitting machines), some hand-knitted—ranging in price from £25 to £75. Occasionally, unique hand-spun and hand-knitted garments are available from £100 to £120. The most traditional sweater is the simple Black Welsh shepherd's sweater, made from the raw wool sheared the previous summer, and is waterproof because the wool retains its natural oils. Made from the wool of the rare pedigreed Black Welsh Mountain sheep, the wool is actually a very dark russet-black that has its own name in Welsh: *Rhuddem.*

Discontinued designs and samples in knitwear are discounted up to 40 percent.

In addition to these two major crafts sources, the Craft Design Centre of Wales exhibits and sells the work of many artisans who make one-of-a-kind pieces.

Roger and Janet Quilter
Penpompren
Rhydcymerau
Nr. Llandeilo
Dyfed SA19 7PP
Tel. (05583) 514

By appointment
Traveler's checks in pounds,
  foreign currency
Mail order

Roger and Janet Quilter make the most imaginative quilts, wall hangings, cushions, and vests that I have seen in Britain or in the northeastern United States. Their designs are sophisticated figurative art, with a wide range of colors and tones that require over 200 different fabrics in the Quilters' palette.

Most of the Quilters' work is one of a kind; some designs are repeated with changes of color and detail. The Quilters will work to order, using the customer's preferred color combination. Wall hangings and nursery quilts take about three weeks, cushion covers about a week, and vests about ten days. Allow more time for Christmas orders, beginning in late September.

In the Quilters' recent collection, a Punch and Judy

nursery quilt or wall hanging measuring 2 by 3 feet and selling for £80 was a knockout, with its brightly striped stage, Punch in the traditional red jester's cap, wielding a stick, Judy in a white-collared blue dress and white mobcap, and a black-and-white spotted dog in a red ruff in front of the stage. It's an incredible piece of work!

Camarthen Landscape, a 4- by 4-foot wall hanging depicting the lovely Welsh countryside in shades of greens, browns, blues, and golds, sells for £100. Local Landscape pillows measuring 18 by 18 inches and using the same palette, are £20, as is a charming pillow of Postman Pat, a favorite children's TV and book character, caught in the act of delivering a kitten to a child living in Rhydcymerau, the Quilters' home.

Among the Quilters' vests, I liked the children's vest of Humpty-Dumpty balancing on his wall for £30, and a woman's vest showing 1920s flappers for £40.

Studio in the Church
Nr. Login
Whitland
Dyfed SA34 0XA
Tel. (09912) 676

Mon.–Fri. 10:00–5:00
Mar.–Christmas; also by
appointment
VISA/Barclaycard,
MasterCard/Access,
traveler's checks in pounds,
U.S. dollars

Alan Hemmings, a hand weaver since the 1950s, specializes in weaving mohair and wool accessories on traditional wooden looms. His Studio in the Church is on a 5th-century site last rebuilt in the 18th century. In Britain, Hemmings supplies one of London's most exclusive shops: the General Trading Company in Sloane Street. Of course, his prices are much lower at his studio.

Hemmings draws his inspiration from this part of western Wales, on the edge of the Preseli Mountains.

His palette features grays, fawns, browns, and greens, highlighted by strong, bright blues and golds, lavender, and rust. His calf-length cloak for £84 is romantic and warm. Accessories include a fringed 46- by 46-inch shawl, which works as well folded into a triangle, for £41.95; a hand-fringed 23- by 57-inch stole for £25.95; a hand-fringed 6- by 57-inch scarf for £8.95; a 7- by 72-inch maxiscarf for £14; a tam-o'-shanter for £8.95; and a larger, puffier artist's beret for £11.

GWENT

Pandy Craft Shop *Mon.–Sun. 8:00–5:30*
Pandy Play Pals *Traveler's checks in pounds*
Ty Newydd Farm *Mail order*
Pandy
Abergavenny
Gwent NP7 8DW
Tel. (0873) 890 235

The most charming animal character dolls are made by Jean and William Hanbury-Evans in a valley just north of the historic market town of Abergavenny. Fine wool flannel from this area dresses many of the creatures, who are clad in traditional Welsh costumes, including national dress.

The marvelous Mouse Family is one of my favorites. Mostyn Mouse is an enormous fellow in the uniform of the Welsh Guards, perfect down to the leek cockade in his bearskin shako. He's a delight, and well worth £27. (He costs $60 *wholesale* in the United States, and $125 retail.) Megan Mouse wears the traditional Welsh woman's outfit—the famous lace-trimmed black hat, and lace collar, cuffs, and apron over a checked wool flannel dress. She costs £25. Morgan Mouse, their son, sports a black-and-white striped shirt, red-and-black checked suspenders, and black pants. He costs £19. Mel Mouse, his younger and smaller brother, wears a red flannel shirt and red-and-black checked overalls, costs £12, as does his sister, Myra Mouse, in lace-trimmed pink-and-white-checked gingham.

Tom Mole, another charmer, is dressed like a miner, with a roguish red bandana around his neck. He and his wife, dressed in a yellow-and-white-checked gingham dress and mobcap, sell for £20 each. A smartly uniformed Policeman Panda also sells for £20.

No collection would be complete without teddy bears, and Pandy Play Pals has some enchanting creatures. Gramps Bear heads the Bear Family in his charcoal chalkstripe overalls and sells for £19. Accompanying him is Granma Bear, whose pert striped chapeau matches her skirt. She sells for £20. Among the grandchildren are Brookie Bear (£19) and the smaller Wayne Bear (£12), in their overalls; Betsy Bear (£20), in her lace-trimmed floral-patterned hooded cape and dress; and Tina Teddy Bear (£12), in a flowered party dress with a flirtatious bow over one ear.

The Pandy Craft Shop sometimes carries samples at reduced prices, as well as story books by Jean Hanbury-Evans that feature the animal characters. Pandy Play Pals welcomes special requests for costumes in specific colors and styles to coordinate with a child's favorite outfit or the color scheme of a room.

GWYNEDD

Llanbedrog Pottery and Prints

The Pottery
Llanbedrog
Pwllheli
Gwynedd L153 7UA
Tel. (0758) 740296

Mon.–Sat. 9:00–9:00 in summer; Mon.–Sat. 9:00–5:00 in winter ("best to telephone first") Traveler's checks, personal checks with ID, foreign currency

Janet Jones is a potter; her husband, Berwyn, is a printmaker. Both have workshops and showrooms at The Pottery.

Her specialties are ginger jars, teapots, and jugs ranging in size from half-pint jugs at £3.85 to 24-inch-high pitchers for £60. Her pots come in subtle shades of green, with a celadon glaze; browns and blacks, with a Japanese *tenmoku* (dark brown) glaze; and white and pink, with a dolomite glaze. Her painstaking techniques require nearly six weeks from the time a pot or jug is first thrown to the time it is glazed and finished.

Rhoscolyn Knitwear

"Tyn Rhos"
Rhoscolyn
Holyhead
Gwynedd LL65 2SJ
Tel. (0407) 860861

Tues.–Sat. 9:30–5:00
Apr.–Sept.; plus Sun.
1:00–5:00 June–Aug.
Traveler's checks in pounds
No mail order, but will ship
purchases

Pam Webb does a lovely collection of original designs in sweaters and accessories made from natural undyed wool produced only on the Isle of Anglesey. Rhoscolyn is located only 4 miles from Holyhead, where you can take the ferry across the Irish Sea from Wales to Ireland.

Prices for men's and women's sweaters range from £26.95 to £36.95. Among the most unusual and attractive patterns are Welsh Castles, with a border of ocean waves and Prince of Wales feathers; the Shepherds Crooks, with a long diagonal pattern within which are the Welsh symbols of daffodils and leeks; Mountain Sheep, bordered by small shepherds' crooks and fences; and Celtic Design, with intertwined motifs and harps. In solids, the Anglesey Pullover is a best bet in navy, cream, black Welsh, or gray Welsh. Men's sweaters cost £36.95, and women's, £34.95. Children's sweaters are also available.

Scarves and hats that coordinate with the sweater patterns cost around £10 to £15. A ribbed scarf in black Welsh wool with pockets to keep hands warm is a clever idea.

A small selection of odds and ends (called oddments) is always available. Prices may be discounted as much as 50 percent.

PEMBROKESHIRE

H. Griffiths & Son
Tregwynt Woollen Mill
Letterston
Haverfordwest
Pembrokeshire SA62 5UX
Tel. (03485) 225

Mon.–Sat. 9:00–5:00
American Express,
*   VISA/Barclaycard,*
*   MasterCard/Access,*
*   traveler's checks in pounds*
*   and U.S. dollars*
Mail order

Tregwynt Mill is located in a picturesque wooded valley 5 miles from Fishguard (from where you can take the ferry to Ireland) and 1 mile from the beautiful Pembrokeshire coast. The Griffith family, owners of this mill since 1912, suggest visiting the mill and shopping, then picnicking on the nearby beaches at Abermawr and Aberbach.

Tregwynt's pure Welsh wool tapestry quilts work well in traditional formal, country, and modern rooms. Fringed on three sides, they come in several sizes—72 by 90 inches (£46), 90 by 100 inches (£54), 100 by 100 inches (£60), and 100 by 120 inches (£75)—in 30 different color combinations, ranging from classics and neutrals to pastels, including three lilac, eight white, and three apricot combinations. Matching cushion covers are £7.50, and throw cushions, £5.25. Children's bedspreads are £12.50, while large throws are £26.70.

A tapestry fabric with a smaller pattern repeat is

used for smaller gift items, like place mats (£1.15 and £1.60) and oven gloves (£4), and the traditional bright colors have been complemented by a new softer pastel palette.

Fabrics are available, too. Pure Welsh wool flannels are 56 inches wide and sell for £8.90 per yard. Tweeds are the same width and cost £9.90 per yard. Tapestry fabrics are 59 inches wide and sell for £15.50 per yard; raised coating fabrics in the same width sell for £11.80 per yard.

Tregwynt Textiles also has branches in Fishguard, about 5 miles to the east (see p. 206), and in St. Davids, about 10 miles to the southwest (see p. 208).

Paul Môrafon Pewter

By appointment
Cash only

Kerrigwyn
Rectory Road
Llangwm
Haverfordwest
Pembrokeshire SA62 4JA
Tel. (0437) 891318

Paul Môrafon designs and makes beautiful hand-embossed pewter picture frames, mirrors, brooches, and small boxes.

His smallest picture frames—2½ by 3 inches—in Celtic Knot, Violet, and Oval patterns cost £10.90. The double Oval frame is priced at £16.60. One of the prettiest small frames has a heart-shaped opening and also costs £10.90; a completely plain 4¼ - by 4½ -inch frame sells for £10.50.

My favorites are the Classic line, in which the picture openings are outlined with a handsome braided design, reminiscent of a laurel wreath. The 2½ - by 3-inch frame is £10.90; the two-picture 3- by 5-inch frame, £16.60; the 4- by 5½-inch frame, £18.90; and the two-picture 5½- by 8¼-inch frame, £26.20.

Brooches come in a variety of Celtic, animal, floral, and astrological designs. Small (1-inch-diameter) brooches are £3.80; medium (1½-inch-diameter) brooches, £4.80; and large (1¾-inch-diameter) brooches, £5.80. Old-fashioned tobacco tins with hinged lids, which could double as stud boxes or pill-boxes, cost only £5.50. The most attractive designs are Celtic Knot, Honeysuckle, Cockerel, and Tapestry Flower.

Tregwynt Textiles
6 High Street
Fishguard
Pembrokeshire
Tel. 872370

Mon.–Sat. 9:00–5:00
American Express,
VISA/Barclaycard,
MasterCard/Access,
traveler's checks in pounds
and U.S. dollars
Mail order

This shop is a branch of Tregwynt Woollen Mill in Letterston, Haverfordwest, about 5 miles to the west. See p. 206 for a complete write-up.

Tregwynt Textiles
5 Nun Street
St. Davids
Pembrokeshire
Tel. 720386

Mon.–Sat. 9:00–5:00
American Express,
VISA/Barclaycard,
MasterCard/Access,
traveler's checks in pounds
and U.S. dollars
Mail order

This shop is a branch of Tregwynt Woollen Mill in Letterston, Haverfordwest, about 10 miles to the northeast. See p. 206 for a complete write-up.

Powys

Plas Robin Products

The Chapel
Pool Road
Montgomery
Powys SY15 6LQ
Tel. (068) 681 459

Mon.–Fri. 9:00–5:00
American Express,
  VISA/Barclaycard,
  MasterCard/Access,
  traveler's checks in pounds
  or dollars, U.S. dollars

Mail Order:
Llandyssil
Montgomery
Powys SY15 6LQ

Plas Robin makes beautiful, original hand-printed textile gifts for the home and garden in pure natural fibers. (Linings may be synthetic, but they are needed for insulated items.)

Nature Trail is one of Plas Robin's newest lines. Taken from hand-engraved wood blocks, the owl, cat, otter, and kingfisher designs are printed onto 100 percent cotton for tea towels (£2), aprons (£4), and tote bags (£5).

Herb-filled plate holders protect your fingers from hot plates while adding their fragrance to your kitchen and dining room. In oak leaf, lavender bush, and currant patterns, they cost only £1.80.

This England is a beautiful pattern, a series of designs extolling the fields, hedges, and wildlife summed up in Shakespeare's famous speech. The color combinations are pink and green, orange and green, or orange and brown on a cream background. Prices range from £1.20 for napkins and £1.50 for plate holders to £5.50 for large aprons and medium tea cosies and £6.50 for the tall coffee cozy. Montgomery, a similar range of products with similar prices, depicts the national emblems of Wales—the dragon and the leek—in burgundy and fawn on cream.

Gardeners will enjoy the large apron patterned with oak leaves and acorns, with pockets labeled TWINE, SEEDS, and KNIFE in a charming Victorian typeface—all for only £6.50, the matching tool bag for £3.20, and the matching foam-padded vinyl-backed garden kneeler for £6.50.

For anyone—and especially for gifts—the bottle bag is a great idea. The bag stands upright and is made to hold one (£2), two (£3.20), or three (£3.90) bottles and/or thermos flasks very comfortably.

Among some of the newer items, in a variety of prints, are a book bag for £3.80, a knitting bag for £5.95, a travel documents case for £3.90, an eyeglass case for £2, and a lingerie case for £5.

Part Five

Ireland

Chapter 17 *Ireland: The Basics*

It's no surprise that most Americans are familiar with the verdant glories of Ireland. There are 45 million Irish-Americans living in the United States, that is, 9 people for every Irish person living in Ireland. Americans receive an especially warm welcome in Ireland, whose slogan is "Ireland of the Welcomes," because just about every Irish person they meet has a brother, sister, or cousin living somewhere in America.

Irish hospitality is famed the world over, and Irish pubs, with Guinness at the source, Irish stories, and Irish music, are a delight.

Savvy shoppers will enjoy Irish fashion and crafts at bargain prices. Here, perhaps more than in other countries of the British Isles, I recommend buying direct from the source. Too many "Ye Olde Crafte Shoppes" trade on tourists' emotional ties to Ireland and their desire to buy Irish products and crafts. And too many tourists, especially Americans, tend to buy feverishly, rather than sensibly, for no other rational reason than "because it's Irish."

Many Irish-made products are indeed lovely, and buying them intelligently will let you get more for your money.

What to Buy

Clothing, especially knitwear and designer garments; natural-fiber luxury fabrics, like Donegal tweeds; yarns; linens; china and pottery; and crystal.

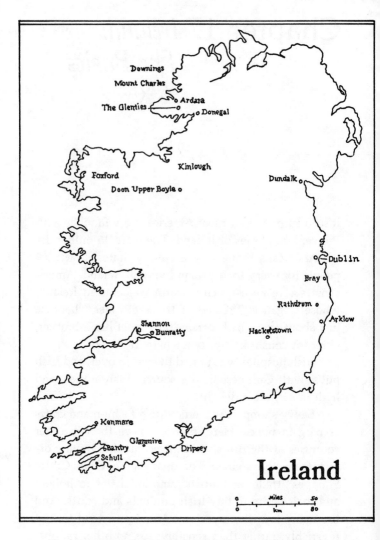

Ireland

Owing to size limitations, the dozens of counties in
Ireland couldn't be included here. Dublin, Shannon,
and Donegal make good bases from which to tour.

1986 Currency Range

The Irish pound (called punt) has not traded on a par with the British pound for several years. The 1986 trading range was £1=$1.24–$1.40, a more favorable rate of exchange than the U.S. dollar to the British pound—made even more favorable by the 8 percent currency devaluation announced in August 1986. In general, prices in Ireland are lower than in Britain, so careful tourists should be able to do well despite their year-long loss of purchasing power abroad.

The VAT

Ireland has three VAT rates: exempt, 10 percent, and 25 percent. Tourist items that are exempt from VAT are clothes and shoes for children from birth to ten years. In the 10-percent category are all adult clothing excluding furs. The maximum 25-percent bracket covers "luxury items": carpets, pottery, glass and crystal, toys, furs, cosmetics, and many other products that are not likely to be bought by tourists. At least the 35-percent VAT rate was abolished in 1985!

Getting It Back

Most shops require a £50 minimum purchase, which can be made up of several items, and many shops will refund the VAT on your credit-card account if you ask the salesperson to do so. VAT refunds on purchases you ship home are automatic, but then you have to pay for shipping and wait six to eight weeks to receive them. The shop may deduct £2 as a processing fee. This refund procedure will save you the bother of getting a check for £8 or £10 several months later, which your bank will charge you $10 or so for cashing, leaving you with only $2 or $3.

I feel that going through the VAT refund procedure makes sense only on large purchases—when the refund will be at least £15, preferably £20. Otherwise, in terms of time and paperwork, it just doesn't seem to pay.

If you plan to take your purchases with you, remember to get an invoice from the shop showing its name and address and the VAT you have paid. *Keep these invoices carefully in your hand baggage*—you'll have to present them for stamping to a customs officer at the airport or port of exit. You should also have those purchases with you, not packed away in your luggage. The customs officer may want to see them to make sure that they are being exported.

When the invoice has been stamped by customs, mail it back to the shop before you leave Ireland. If you have used a credit card, the shop will make the refund, less any handling charge, when it receives the invoice, by crediting your credit-card account.

TELEPHONE NUMBERS

The telephone numbers given for the shops show both the city area code and the telephone number. If you are dialing from within the same city, omit the area code, which is the number in parentheses. If you are dialing from outside the city, include it. If you are dialing from outside the country—for example, from the United States or Canada—start with the international access code (011), followed by the code for Ireland (353), followed by the city code (the number in parentheses *minus the zero*). Thus a call from New York to Dublin would begin 011 353 1. But a call from Shannon to Dublin would begin 01.

Chapter 18 *Dublin*

"In Dublin's fair city," the old song begins, and Dublin is indeed fair, made for the visitor who enjoys exploring cities on foot. And there is much to explore. You'll want to see the landmark Georgian buildings with their colorfully painted doors, immortalized in the delightful poster *The Doors of Dublin*. The sixth-century *Book of Kells* in the library of Trinity College is such a treasure that the curators open it to a different page periodically, lest any one page become damaged by light.

If the Abbey Theatre, the Peacock (a little theater in the same building), or the Gate Theatre is in season, you are in for a rare and inexpensive treat. The best seats are only about £10, and you'll see superb theater, with plays by Synge, O'Casey, Behan, and other Irish playwrights.

When it comes to shopping, the Powerscourt Townhouse Centre in Clarendon Street, near Grafton Street, has gotten a great deal of publicity as Dublin's version of Ghirardelli Square, the Quincy Market, and the South Street Seaport. It's an accurate description, but hardly a favorable one as far as serious shoppers are concerned. Like its American counterparts, the Powerscourt Townhouse Centre is a wonderful place to stroll and take in the surroundings or to have coffee and a snack or a drink and enjoy the passing scene. But it's not for serious shopping. The prices are too high. About the only exception is John Rocha, whose couture

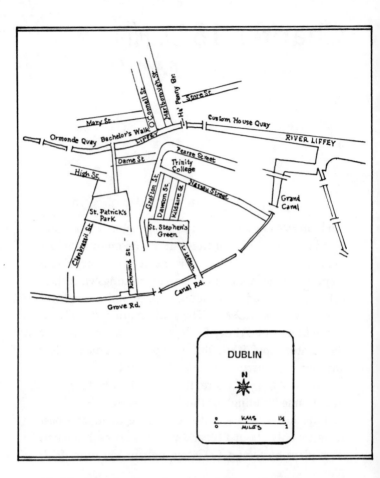

Dublin's main shopping area is marvelously
compact; but with so many wonderful things to buy,
you'll need at least two days to cover the territory.

clothing for women—under the label Chinatown Clothing—is a relatively good buy.

Instead, for under-one-roof shopping, the IDA Enterprise Centre in Pearse Street is a far better source of crafts bargains, with over a dozen artisans' workshops and showrooms. You'll do better enjoying the fun at Powerscourt, then doing your shopping at the IDA Enterprise Centre.

Dublin, the city that delighted George Bernard Shaw, James Joyce, Sean O'Casey, Oscar Wilde, and Jonathan Swift, will enchant you, too.

Cleo Ltd.

18 Kildare Street
Dublin 2
Tel. (01) 761421 or
611752

*Mon.–Fri. 9:00–5:30, Sat.
9:30–5:00
VISA/Barclaycard, traveler's
checks in pounds, personal
checks with ID
Mail order*

Cleo's Kitty Joyce is the doyenne of Irish couture. She has been designing beautiful garments for women, men, and children in wool and linen hand-knitted and handwoven fabrics and tweeds for over fifty years. The intricacy and subtlety of her palette are reminiscent of Missoni's, but her prices are so much lower! Handwoven wool skirts are £67, and the matching stoles are £23 (45 by 54 inches), £37 (72 by 54 inches), and £46 (90 by 54 inches).

Women's and men's intricately knitted sweaters in smoky shades, bright colors, and the classic Aran white, many trimmed with handmade fossilized bog oak or pottery buttons, range from £72.50 to £95.50. Children's sweaters start at £31.50. For the do-it-yourselfer, hand-knitting yarns are £11 per ½ kilogram, suiting tweeds are £20.20 per meter, and coating tweeds are £25.40 per meter. Charming one-of-a-kind hand-knitted teddy bears sporting hand-knitted sweaters are only £8.

Don't miss Cleo's permanent sale rack, full of samples and garments from the previous season's line. On a recent trip I found tweed coats for £70 to £100, tweed jackets for £50 to £60, and tweed skirts for only £20. Many sizes were small, but stock changes very frequently.

If you're down in the southwest, visit Cleo's shop at 2 Shelbourne Street, Kenmare, Co. Kerry, about 20 miles south of Killarney (see p. 239).

Pat Crowley

14 Duke Street
Dublin 2
Tel. (01) 710219

Mon.–Fri. 9:30–6:00, Sat.
9:30–5:00
American Express,
VISA/Barclaycard,
traveler's checks in pounds,
personal checks with ID

Pat Crowley's classy, dashing couture appears frequently in *Town and Country* magazine. She designs lovely garments in wool tweeds, linens, and silks for the local and international racing set, who come to Ireland for the bloodstock sales. Pat caters to individuals and does a great deal of custom work.

Her prices for tweed suits start at around £300, for silk dresses at around £300, for more tailored linen dresses at £249, and for linen blazers at £159. Linen blouses with pin tucking and lace begin at £129.

Pat Crowley specializes in two very different types of looks: classic sportswear with a feminine touch for day, and the knock-'em-dead sensuous, romantic big-evening dress, starting at £400.

Pat's basement markdowns are the reason she is in this book. Cash flow is the name of the game, and leftover pieces from her collections go on sale early and often at unbelievably low prices. Donegal tweed suits in mossy green or tobacco were marked down from £300 to £120, silk dresses were reduced from £300 to £50–£100, and evening dresses were reduced from £400–£450 to only £100.

Dublin Woollen Mills

41 Lower Ormond Quay
Dublin 1
Tel. (01) 775014 or
770301

Mon.–Sat. 9:00–5:30
American Express,
*   VISA/Barclaycard,*
*   MasterCard/Access,*
*   traveler's checks in pounds*
Mail order

The Dublin Woollen Mills, for which James Joyce was once a terrible sales representative, is just over the enchanting little Ha'penny Bridge—the first footbridge over the River Liffey—upriver from the O'Connell Bridge. The Dublin Woollen Mills, celebrating its centennial in 1988, offers low prices and an excellent variety of merchandise.

If you're not going up to Donegal for woolens, there's an excellent selection of tweeds here, with great bargains in remnants. I bought a John McNutt (see p. 238) mustard tweed remnant large enough for a stole or cape for only £10.

Jimmy Hourihan's tweed jackets for women were £72.50—lower than I've seen them elsewhere—and Richard Malcolm's fine wool blouses in cream, rose, or Wedgwood blue were £36.50 here, compared to £39.50, the next lowest price I'd seen them, at Avoca Handweavers (see p. 245). Pretty hand-knitted mohair sweaters in a rainbow of solid colors and patterns were on sale at £59.50 for crewneck sweaters and £62.50 for V-neck sweaters. Aran sweaters were priced at £30 for hand-loomed sweaters, made on hand-knitting machines, and £50–£60 for hand-knitted sweaters.

Beautiful men's tweed jackets were priced at £87.50. Hand-loomed Aran sweaters were £30, and hand-knitted Aran sweaters, £50–£60. Men's tweed and leather slippers were £19.75.

Children's hand-knitted Aran sweaters ranged from £22.50 for the 20-inch newborn size to £38.50 for the 32-inch size. For the hand-knitter, white or gray Bainin yarn, used in Aran sweaters, costs 75p for a 50-gram ball, or £14.80 per kilogram, which will make one adult or two children's sweaters.

Failte Crystal

The Tower
IDA Enterprise Centre
Pearse Street
Dublin 2
Tel. (01) 775655

Mon.–Fri. 9:00–5:30
American Express,
VISA/Barclaycard,
MasterCard/Access,
traveler's checks in
pounds
No mail order, but will send
purchases

Failte—Gaelic for "welcome"—Crystal specializes in intaglio engraving of its emblem, the Marlay Rose, which is found in Marlay Park in the foothills of the Dublin Mountains. The rose pattern is composed of 24 painstakingly placed cuts, done entirely freehand, and each 27-percent lead crystal piece is signed and dated by the individual craftsman who made it.

In stemware, the champagne flute, at £13, and the large goblet, at £15, are good buys. The petite violet vase for £9 is charming, as are the bud vase and the posy vase, each for £12. The salad bowl for £45, the square decanter for £80, and the ship's decanter for £100 are large and impressive.

Failte Crystal will also engrave your monogram or logo.

Kapp & Peterson Ltd.

Pipe Makers
117 Grafton Street
Dublin 2
Tel. (01) 714652

Mon.–Sat. 9:30–5:30
American Express,
*   VISA/Barclaycard,*
*   MasterCard/Access,*
*   traveler's checks in pounds*
Mail order

Kapp & Peterson is a world-famous pipemaker, with a branch in Old Bond Street, London. This charming old shop, the largest tobacconist in Dublin, is the only source of traditional clay pipes (£5.25) I could find. It has the best selection of pipes, tobaccos, and cigars in Dublin. Beautiful briar "rejects" are £4.25, and there is an excellent selection of pipes at £8.50–£30.

Get your Cuban cigars here, but make sure that you smoke them before you return to the United States, where they are subject to confiscation by customs.

Sheleen

Handcrocheted Garments and
*   Separates*
28 Cypress Park
Templeogue
Dublin 6
Tel. (01) 903594

Mon.–Fri. 9:00–5:00
Traveler's checks in pounds,
*   U.S. dollars, personal*
*   checks with ID*
Mail order—preferably from
*   previous customers or*
*   visitors*

Sheila Church runs what she calls a "cottage industry" from her home in Dublin, but it's a cottage industry that sells to Saks Fifth Avenue and Neiman-Marcus in the United States, which, in turn, charge much higher prices than those Mrs. Church charges her visitors.

Sheleen quotes prices in U.S. dollars, which makes

it easy to see what bargains the designs are. Beautiful hand-crocheted shawls and stoles in cotton, fine wool, or mohair range from $33 to $40. The Irish Rose shawl, which is the most intricate and expensive at $40, features individual roses that are crocheted into the shawl petal by petal. The christening shawl at $35.50 is sure to become an heirloom, along with the christening robe for only $75.

There is a lovely collection in cotton and linen crochet. An Edwardian blouse in white or black costs $105, with a matching or contrasting Irish Rose skirt for $150. Together, in white, they would make a lovely romantic wedding or summer evening dress; in black, they'd make a dramatic evening dress for all seasons. Hand-crocheted collars cost only $20; crocheted cotton blouses, $45 and $50; and crocheted linen tops, $55.

Sheleen does beautiful wool and mohair sweaters. The Colleen sweater, made of mohair with a contrasting-color triangular front panel, comes in black/turquoise, black/gray, or cream/beige for only $75. The Mohair Glengarry jacket is available in autumn shades of rust/cream/sage green and four other striking color combinations for $85. Sheleen also designs charming mohair vests for $45 and $48.

Other pretty sweaters are the Aran Glengarry cardigan with a deep V neck in natural wool for $65.50, a Celtic leaf sweater in natural or colored wool for $62, the Aran crocheted sweater with cable stitch in white, royal, aqua, or red wool for only $50, and the checkerboard three-quarter-length shawl-collared cardigan in navy, black, or royal with white for $70.

There is also a wide selection of vests for $40 to $48, including two men's designs for $43.50 and $45. In addition, there are nine styles of women's hats, priced at $10.50 each.

Wooden Wonders
The Tower
IDA Enterprise Centre
Pearse Street
Dublin 2
Tel. (01) 775655

Mon.–Fri. 9:00–5:30
Traveler's checks in pounds,
*   U.S. dollars, British*
*   pounds*
Mail order under
*   consideration—send inquiry*

Wooden Wonders makes charming children's jigsaw puzzles—painted in nontoxic colors—at incredibly low prices. They are designed to teach colors, shapes, language, numbers, and geography and to improve coordination, concentration, and memory. The puzzles include jigsaw maps of Ireland, with its counties and towns, available in both English and Gaelic, as well as maps of Europe, England, Wales, and Scotland. These complex maps cost only £9.95.

Puzzles for younger children—ten-piece pictures of a farm or the seaside—are priced at £5.95. The farm scene, for children three to six years of age, has a pig, a duck, a rooster, a hen, a cat, a cow, a sheep, a farmer with his piglet, the farmer's wife on a tractor, and a scarecrow in the field behind her. There's certainly a lot of activity and learning experience in the puzzle. For toddlers, five-piece puzzles of teddy bears, elephants, honey bears, and trains are only £2.95.

A bargain box contains discontinued merchandise: maps for £7, ten-piece puzzles for £4, and small puzzles for only £2.

If you are a parent or grandparent or have young relatives or friends, you'll find wonderful gifts at Wooden Wonders.

Chapter 19 *The Rest of Ireland*

Dublin is exciting, but it's only a small part of Ireland —even though it accounts for one-quarter of Ireland's population. To really know Ireland, you must get out into the beautiful countryside. If your time is limited, you can still visit the romantic Vale of Avoca and the Wicklow Mountains just an hour's drive south of Dublin.

Ranging even farther, if time permits, visit the glorious west—the Dingle peninsula and bay, the River Shannon, and the burren country, where wild-flowers grow amid a limestone landscape. Seeing the sun go down on Galway Bay is a treat as beautiful as the old Irish song. And, if you can, visit the magnificent rugged country of Donegal in Ireland's far north-west.

As you'll see in the following pages, the shopping is wonderful. Getting around the countryside is best by car; but if you'd rather be driven around so that you can enjoy the scenery, the CIE—Ireland's national transport authority—has an excellent Mainline rail and Expressway bus system to all parts of Ireland, for which Dublin is a major hub. If you plan to cover a lot of territory, CIE offers weekly and monthly passes similar to the BritRail pass and Eurailpass that are bargains.

County Carlow

Honeysuckle Products
Kelvin Bolt Ltd.
The Water Mill
Hacketstown
County Carlow
Tel. (0508) 71375

Mon.–Fri. 9:00–5:30 (a phone call before visiting is advised)
Traveler's checks in pounds, foreign currency
Mail order—catalogs available in showroom; can be mailed direct to the United States for $2.00

This restored 250-year-old water mill, complete with working water wheel, carries an enormous selection of beautifully packaged and inexpensive culinary and medicinal herbs, herbal sleep pillows, sachets, herbal bath bags, essential oils, herb seeds, and a variety of herbal gifts and books.

Honeysuckle sells a multitude of herbs, from allspice to vanilla pods, for just pennies per ounce—much cheaper than in the United States. Cinnamon sticks are only 6p each, licorice roots 7p each, whole nutmegs 8p each, and vanilla pods 30p each. The shop even carries such exotica as crystallized angelica for 50p per ounce and Chinese five-spice mixture for 35p per ounce. There are 50–60 medicinal herbs at comparably low prices.

Handmade herbal sleep pillows are lovely and soothing. The Elizabethan sleep pillow sells for £4.85. Measuring 8 by 10 inches, it is made of lace-edged, delicately patterned fabric and comes filled with hops, basil, and mint or with rose and lavender. The hop pillow and rose and lavender pillow also come packaged with a lace-edged, heart-shaped lavender sachet for £5.60. The Victorian sleep pillow is a 5- by 11-inch cylinder covered in a delicate floral striped fabric and is filled with rose and lavender or with lemon verbena. It costs £7.95.

Honeysuckle carries a whole range of sachets that make lovely small gifts. The lace-topped luxury linen sachet for £2.20 and the standard linen sachet in a tweedy fabric for £1.75 come in lavender, rose, or southernwood. Boy or girl lavender doll sachets cost £1.75. Lace-edged potpourri sachets sell for £2.25, and sachets covered on one side in hand-crocheted white lace in lavender or rose sell for £3.45.

Herbal bath bags are delightful. Each bath bag contains a blend of herbs and essences—no artificial ingredients or detergents—and will last for three baths. Each set of bath bags contains an assortment of blends: chamomile/rosemary/lavender, peppermint/rosemary /horsetail, and thyme/lavender. Choose from the Bath Bag Basket—nine bath bags in a basket with a wash-cloth—for £8.75; the Bath Bag Box—nine bath bags in an acetate gift box—for £7.50; or the Bath Bag Sack— eight bath bags in a hand-printed cotton sack—for £5.50.

Honeysuckle also makes natural herbal and floral perfumes and packages them in 25-cc bottles for £2.95. Elizabethan is a delicate blend of natural flower oils, Woodland is a green scent of flowers and aromatic woodland plants, Old English has the aroma of an old-fashioned English garden, and Lavender and Poppy are self-evident. Foaming bath oils come in two scents: Cill Uisce, a citrus scent for mornings, and Cill Dara, a flowery evening scent. Both come in 150-cc bottles and cost only £1.90.

Honeysuckle Products carries many other lovely things. It's definitely worth a visit.

COUNTY CLARE

Ballycasey Craft Centre

Shannon
County Clare
Tel. (061) 62105

Artists' hours and credit-card policies vary. Please see each listing for details.

Located just 3 miles from Shannon Airport, Ballycasey Craft Centre houses a marvelous selection of crafts workers in a restored 18th-century stable block. All the work here is of extremely high quality and excellent design. Definitely worth a visit.

Lucy Erridge

Knitwear Designer
Unit 1D
Ballycasey Craft Centre
Shannon
County Clare
Tel. (061) 74617

Mon.–Sat. 9:00–5:00
VISA/Barclaycard,
MasterCard/Access,
traveler's checks in pounds

Lucy Erridge produces some of the most elegant, sophisticated, and wearable sweaters, dresses, and suits I've seen anywhere. Lucy will also do made-to-measure garments and special color combinations for customers —a very rare and welcome service. Prices run around £200, including the 10-percent refundable VAT, but samples from the previous season are much less. Great buys were a pink silk suit marked down from £200 to £80, a rust linen suit marked down from £230 to £120, and a series of camel and cream suits trimmed with leather reduced from £200 to £80.

Brian R. Gleeson
Goldsmith/Designer
Ballycasey Craft Centre
Shannon
County Clare
Tel. (061) 74115

Mon.–Sat. 9:00–5:30; Sun.
in June–Aug. 9:00–5:30
American Express,
VISA/Barclaycard,
MasterCard/Access,
traveler's checks in pounds

Brian Gleeson produces unusual jewelry in 9- and 18-karat gold and in sterling silver, much of it inspired by local flora. His pieces start as low as £30 and go up to over £2,000 (prices include the refundable 25-percent VAT, so are really 20 percent lower), with a wide selection in each price range. Floral earrings with 18-karat golden petals and a single cabochon ruby, emerald, or sapphire sell for £65–£75. A hammered heavy 18-karat gold torque (a rigid V-shaped necklace) costs £200, and a spectacular ruby and diamond necklace costs £1,500. Most pieces are one of a kind, with special emphasis on engagement rings and wedding bands. Brian will also design to order.

Rineanna Pottery
Handthrown Earthenware
Ballycasey Craft Center
Shannon
County Clare
Tel. (061) 62105

Mon.–Sat. 10:00–6:00; Sun.
by appointment
Traveler's checks in pounds

Max Halliday's pottery is unbelievably inexpensive. Unusual glazed candlesticks are only £5! Glazed rust and white salad sets—a large bowl and six smaller ones—are only £38. Fifteen-piece coffee sets—a pot, sugar, creamer, and six cups and saucers are £52 in a black glaze and £47.50 in a white glaze. His designs fit in beautifully with country or modern decor.

Ballycar Design
Ballycasey Craft Centre
Shannon
County Clare
Tel. (061) 62105

Mon.–Sat. 10:00–5:00
VISA/Barclaycard, traveler's
checks in pounds
Mail order

Patchwork and sampler kits are the specialties here. Pure linen sampler kits designed by the owners sell for £9 to £16, depending on the size and complexity. Patchwork cushion covers in silk, cotton, or a mixture of pieces in both fabrics range from £14 to £26.

Vonnie Reynolds
Bunratty Cottage
Opposite Bunratty Castle
Bunratty County Clare
Tel. (061) 74321

Mon.–Sat. 9:00–5:30
American Express,
VISA/Barclaycard,
MasterCard/Access,
traveler's checks in pounds

Vonnie Reynolds's designs, primarily in Donegal tweed, are but a few of the items she carries in her very upscale, tourist-oriented shop. Her own designs, which reportedly have been bought by Katharine Hepburn, Vanessa Redgrave, and Jeanne Kirkpatrick, are expensive, but many are worth the money and are certain to be crowd-stoppers. Among them: tweed suits in the £250 range and exquisite Victorian-inspired white, cream, pink, gold, or black silk blouses slathered with silk lace for £234.

However, her prices on Irish linen tablecloths and many other items not originating in her workshop are ludicrous. An oval 72- by 90-inch double damask tablecloth is £125 here (around $171), compared to $82.50 at the Shannon Airport Duty-free Store, where all prices are quoted in dollars. The largest tablecloth, 72 by 126 inches, is £175 here (around $240), compared to $120 at Shannon.

To balance the bad news, there are some items on sale. Especially good buys were a velvet-trimmed tweed suit designed by Vonnie Reynolds's daughter, Marielouise, marked down from £248 to £148, and a rack of tweed skirts, reduced to £49.95.

Note: Because Mrs. Reynolds delivers purchases to your departing flight at Shannon or will ship them home for you, all prices *exclude* VAT.

Shannon Airport Duty-free Store

Shannon Free Airport
Shannon
County Clare
Tel. (061) 62610

Mon.–Sun. 8:00–10:00 in summer; Mon.–Sun. 9:30–5:30 in winter. May be held open if an incoming flight is late. The liquor section and a small section of the shop are open 24 hours.
American Express, Diners Club, VISA/Barclaycard, MasterCard/Access, traveler's checks in pounds, U.S. dollars
Mail order

What can I write about a shop that carries 15,000 items and whose mail-order catalog alone lists 3,000–4,000 items and goes to 4–5 million customers a year! To make things even easier and better, all prices in this enormous shop are quoted in dollars, and tourists have the opportunity to "preshop": to visit the duty-free shop when they arrive and to comparison shop or actually purchase their goods immediately, to be held for their homeward flight. Do take the time to comparison shop, and take notes for major purchases. It will pay off in enormous savings.

The Shannon Airport Duty-free Store, in operation for over thirty years, carries major Irish brands like

Waterford, Cavan Crystal, and Belleek China. It also carries such foreign brands as Orrefors, Limoges, Bing & Grondahl, Wedgwood, Royal Copenhagen (figurines only), Villeroy & Boch, Hummel, Ginori, Noritake, Pringle, Lyle & Scott, and Hermès.

Pure Irish linen damask tablecloths are less expensive here than anywhere in Ireland—except, perhaps, at the factories in Northern Ireland. There are three patterns—Chrysanthemum (my favorite), Shamrock, and Satin Band—and prices range from $52.80 for a 54- by 72-inch rectangle and $71.50 for a 72-inch round up to $134.20 for a 72- by 144-inch banquet-size rectangle. A set of six 22-inch square napkins is $42.90, and a set of eight, $57.20.

Oddly enough, Nottingham lace tablecloths are less expensive here than they are in Nottingham—perhaps because Shannon buys in such great quantities. In white or cream, the Diane floral pattern in 95 percent cotton/5 percent polyester fabric ranges from only $13.75 for a 50-inch round tablecloth and $21.45 for a 50- by 70-inch oval to $48.85 for a 70- by 126-inch rectangle. The Leaf pattern, in the same fabric, ranges from $13.20 for a 50-inch round tablecloth and $31.35 for a 70- by 90-inch oval to $47.35 for a 70- by 126-inch rectangle. A set of eight 12- by 18-inch place mats and a 12- by 36-inch table runner in white or beige costs only $23.

Shannon has a great many special offers. One of the best is a sale on Waterford Crystal in April through October, when many pieces are reduced 20 percent.

Hermès scarves were lower here than anywhere in Ireland or the United Kingdom: $68, compared to £75 (then the equivalent of $105) in Dublin, and priced similarly in London.

Liquor is usually a good bargain, but comparison shop at home first. If your local liquor stores are very competitive, it may not pay for you to drag a bottle home to save only a dollar or two.

County Cork

The Irish Scene Factory Knitwear Shop

Wolfe Tone Square
Bantry
County Cork
Tel. (027) 50606

Mon.–Sat. 9:00–5:30
Traveler's checks, personal
checks with ID
Mail order

The Irish Scene Factory Knitwear Shop—formerly the Designer Knitwear Shop—is located at the headquarters of one of Ireland's fastest-growing designer knitwear companies.

Colorful picture sweaters in pure wool are among the best buys. Ordinarily £39–£45, there are always slightly imperfect sweaters for only £29. Among the prettiest patterns are Irish farmhouses and animals, scenes of Dublin's terraced houses along the River Liffey, and Irish seaside resorts with sailboats and seagulls.

Geometric color-block sweaters in pure wool, made to use up yarn colors from discontinued patterns, are a bargain at £19.50–£29, as are samples and one-of-a-kind sweaters from past seasons, which sell for as little as £19.50.

Dripsey Woollen Mills, Ltd.

Dripsey
Co. Cork
Tel. (021) 445006

Mon.–Fri. 8:30–12:30 and
1:30–5:30, Sun.
2:30–5:00
VISA/Barclaycard
Mail order

Dripsey Woollen Mills, about 14 miles from Cork on the Cork-Killarney road, won eight gold medals at the International Fabrics Exposition in California. Bellville Sassoon used Dripsey tweed for a suit worn by the Princess of Wales last year, and Yves Saint Laurent, Pierre Cardin, and Kenzo often use Dripsey's tweeds and fine wools.

Dripsey takes the wool from fleece to fabric, doing all the dyeing, spinning, and weaving. Besides controlling quality, this vertical integration lowers the price.

Homespun hand-knitted yarns in a rainbow of colors sell for about £6.50 per pound. Three-ply oiled Aran yarn sells for £4.90 per pound. Woolen fabrics—tweeds and fine saxonies and cheviots—in widths of 56 to 60 inches average £8 to £10.50 per yard, with the finer fabrics selling for up to £12 per yard.

Knitwear by Phyllis O'Meara Ltd.

Lissacaha
Schull
Co. Cork
Tel. (028) 28356

Mon.–Sat. 9:00–5:30 and usually later—(phone to make sure of an appointment)
Diners Club, VISA/Barclaycard, MasterCard/Access, personal checks with ID
Mail order

Phyllis O'Meara designs beautiful knitwear in a variety of styles: colorful multicolor sweaters, plain guernsey-type sweaters (please see p. 102 for a full description), knitted suits, and long coats in stained-glass-window designs.

Children's picture sweaters are charming and cost only £18 to £20. Choose from ponies in a field, donkeys, pigs, teddy bears, or a traditional Irish thatched cottage. Sheep pullovers are a bargain at only £15.

Factory-shop prices range from £27.50 for an adult sweater to £70 for a mohair cardigan. Among recent best buys are a Dior check black and white jacket for

£45 and a matching lined skirt for £28. Chunky tweed sweaters in a variety of colors are £40.

Very often the factory shop has bargains—sweaters with tiny flaws or the previous season's designs—for about £20.

Phyllis O'Meara will do name sweaters at no extra charge and can make sweaters with a yacht logo and the name of your boat on the chest for every member of your family.

Morna Crochet Designs

Glanmire
County Cork
Tel. (021) 353 459

Mon.–Sat. 9:00–6:00
American Express (slight
surcharge to cover costs),
traveler's checks in pounds,
foreign currency
Mail order by inquiry

What a treat to find Irish crochet at wholesale prices—especially when retail markups range from 80 to 120 percent!

All Morna Crochet's designs are handmade in 100 percent cotton: suits, dresses, skirts, blouses, collars, place mats (called dinner mats), tea cozies, tablecloths, and bedspreads.

Morna's crocheted blouses are among the prettiest designs. The Rose & Shamrock cardigan with a high mandarin neck, scoop neck, or a V neck costs £75. The Diamond camisole costs £45, and the Diamond blouse with a peplum and a variety of necklines costs £65. An intricate flower-design blouse with long sleeves and a high or V neck costs £79. Evening dresses range from £160 to £179.

Collar and cuff sets sell for £11, and gloves in white, black, or ecru go for £12.50. Christening robes are £45 and £69.

Exquisite scallop-edged 14-inch round place mats sell for £10, and rectangular 10- by 16-inch rosebud-bordered mats cost £11.

Tablecloths and bedspreads are more expensive, but still a bargain compared to retail prices in Dublin and abroad. A 70-inch round rose-patterned tablecloth costs £130, twin bedspreads cost £145 and £175, and doubles cost £175 and £200.

COUNTY DONEGAL

Campbell's of Glenties

Thady Campbell & Co., Ltd.
The Glenties
County Donegal
Tel. (075) 51106

Mon.–Sat. 9:00–6:00
American Express, Diners
Club, VISA/Barclaycard,
MasterCard/Access,
traveler's checks in all
currencies
Mail order—catalog on
request

Campbell's of Glenties has been making fine hand-knitted and hand-loomed sweaters and accessories since 1908.

Sweaters in a variety of Aran patterns start at £20 for hand-loomed garments, made on hand-knitting machines, and go up to £65 for hand-knitted Aran sweaters with intricate patterns.

Campbell's has a great collection of knitted gloves and mittens, socks, caps, hats, and scarves. At about £5 each, they are a real bargain.

Jean's Craft Shop Ltd.

Drumconor
Mount Charles
Co. Donegal
Tel. (073) 35192

Mon.–Sun. 9:00–6:00
Easter–Sept.; Mon.–Fri.
9:00–6:00 Oct.–Easter
American Express,
VISA/Barclaycard,
MasterCard/Access,
traveler's checks in pounds,
foreign currency
Mail order

I find Jean's clothing expensive, but her toys are charming and well priced, especially for their size. The Aran boy, a 14-inch wool sock doll that wears tweed trousers and an Aran sweater and cap, costs £13.50. His sister, same size and price, wears a tweed dress and a crocheted shawl.

Red Riding Hood, another wool sock doll, wears a gingham dress and a crocheted cloak. She is 14 inches high and sells for £13.75.

A 14-inch ram with white yarn fleece and assorted tweed horns is £13.75, and a charming 16-inch tweed teddy bear with velvet paws, ears, and nose is £13.50.

McNutt Weaving Company Ltd.	*Mon.–Sat. 9:00–6:00*
Downings	*Sept.–May; Mon.–Sat.*
County Donegal	*9:00–7:00 June–Aug.*
Tel. (074) 55324	*American Express,*
	VISA/Barclaycard,
	MasterCard/Access,
	traveler's checks in pounds

Donegal is at the northwest corner of Ireland, but if you're a home sewer, this long trip will be more than worth your while. McNutt's exquisite tweeds and linens are featured in the collections of Valentino, Giorgio Armani, Basile, Gianfranco Ferré, Gianni Versace, Escada, Perry Ellis, Claude Montana, and Kenzo, where even a simple skirt can cost $500, and a jacket, over $800.

But at McNutt's retail shop beside its mill, you'll find the same magnificent fabrics, often as remnants or ends of bolts, for around £8–£10 per meter for extra-wide 60-inch fabric.

In addition to tweeds and linens, you'll find natural mixtures, like linen/cotton blends, but no synthetics. "We don't want to touch synthetics!" designer John McNutt's marketing uncle Bill McNutt says forcefully.

If you're not going as far as Donegal but will be in Dublin, check the Dublin Woollen Company (see p.

221), which sometimes carries a small selection of McNutt remnants. On a recent trip, I picked up a piece of caramel tweed large enough for a skirt or giant shawl for only £10.

John Molloy Factory Shop
Killybegs Road
Ardara
County Donegal
Tel. (075) 41133 or 41243
 or 41244

Mon.–Sat. "very long hours" (phone first if in doubt)
American Express, Diners Club, VISA/Barclaycard, MasterCard/Access, traveler's checks in pounds
Mail order

John Molloy, who manufactures Donegal hand-woven tweeds and fashion hand-knitted goods, also owns the Donegal Shop in Letterkenny, but it's his factory shop in Ardara that is interesting because it sells off all of the previous season's knitwear and tweed garments at unbeatable prices. And, of course, for such classic designs, the concept of season is meaningless.

Hand-knitted Aran sweaters start at £40; for hand-knitted sweaters—as opposed to hand-loomed ones, which are made on hand-knitting machines—these prices are among the lowest I've seen anywhere.

Men's Donegal tweed jackets sell for £65, ladies' Donegal tweed jackets for £70, and ladies' Donegal tweed suits for £100. The prices are excellent and the merchandise changes rapidly. Give them a visit.

COUNTY KERRY

Cleo Ltd.
2 Shelbourne Street
Kenmare
County Kerry
Tel. (064) 41410

Mon.–Fri. 9:00–5:30, Sat. 9:30–5:00 Apr.–Oct.
VISA/Barclaycard, traveler's checks in pounds, personal checks with ID
Mail order

The famous Kerry toad emblazons the outside of the County Kerry branch of Cleo's, Irish couture for women, men, and children. Cleo's main shop in Dublin is reviewed on p. 219.

COUNTY LEITRIM

Cottage Handcrafts
Glenade
Kinlough
County Leitrim
Tel. (072) 41470

Mon.–Sat. 9:00–6:00
VISA/Barclaycard,
 MasterCard/Access,
 traveler's checks in pounds,
 U.S. dollars
Mail order

Cottage Handcrafts is hidden away in a tiny valley at the foot of the Dartry Mountains to the east and the Benbulben Mountains to the west, about 20 miles from Sligo City.

The purists at Cottage Handcrafts make their Irish sweaters for men, women, and children completely by hand in creamy white natural wool. The Glenade crew-neck sweater in sizes 34 to 42 inches, with its traditional combination of cables, honeycombs, and diamonds filled in with moss stitch, costs £50; the matching hat is £8. The O'Rourke jacket for women is a classic cardigan with pockets and dark brown buttons. It is made with the same stitches, comes in sizes 34 to 42 inches, and costs £52. For men, the Curragh Bawn crewneck, also made with combinations of the traditional stitches, comes in sizes 38 to 46 inches and costs £56. This sweater is also available as a turtleneck (called a polo neck).

Women's hand-knitted mohair sweaters are new items. Cardigans in fashion shades of lilac, coffee, blue, mulberry, and cream cost £58; hand-knitted mohair stoles are £22.

COUNTY LOUTH

Patricia Murphy
Textile Designer
17 Francis Street
Dundalk
County Louth
Tel. (042) 34037

Mon.–Fri. 10:00–1:00,
2:30–5:30; Sat. by
appointment
MasterCard/Access in process
Traveler's checks in pounds,
personal checks with ID
Mail order

Patricia Murphy is a textile designer and painter who paints her designs on pure natural fabrics—silk, wool, and cotton—which are made into scarves, shawls, and cushions. Her designs are primarily floral and geometric in bright and pastel colors. Each design is limited to small editions; as each piece is hand-painted, each one is unique.

Patricia Murphy's silk scarves are wonderful buys and make imaginative lightweight presents. Her long scarf is 8 by 50 inches and costs only £10. Her 36-inch squares are £25 and £28. Among the square scarves, those with red and yellow tulips and green leaves on a dark blue background with a pale green zigzag and a violet border were standouts, as were those with multicolored tulips on a blue background with a pale green zigzag and a pinkish red panel; blue irises and red tulips with green leaves against a background of black, red, yellow, and blue bands; pink and red tropical flowers on a pale cream background; and blue irises against a blue, green, and pink background. Larger silk shawls measuring 36 by 50 inches for £41 have similar patterns and color combinations, as well as some lovely geometric patterns.

Featherweight wool scarves and shawls come in three sizes: 18- by 50-inch scarves (£20), 45-inch square scarves (£37), and 48- by 54-inch shawls (£60). These are painted in interesting geometric patterns.

The shawls are painted in glowing jewel colors and combine style and individuality in their unique designs.

Some silk scarves from previous seasons have been marked down to super-bargain prices, ranging from £6 to £18.

In addition to these accessories, Patricia Murphy paints pictures on fabric. Small pictures sell for £15–£25, and are one-of-a-kind impressionistic views of Irish scenery: the mountains, the sea, and the wildlife. Larger paintings are more detailed and more costly. *Wild Irish Sea* is painted on cotton and is a 32-inch square showing white-capped pale gray waves against a pale blue and pink sky, a rocky blue and green island, and many-colored birds. It costs £75. Still larger wall hangings are painted on wool, measure 36 by 72 inches, and cost £170. *Vase of Tulips Against the Light* shows pink tulips in an orange vase on a patterned cloth against a dark violet wall and a pink tabletop. *Looking at the Burren* uses a softer, more subtle palette and contrasts a vase of daffodils against a background of burren landscape, with its mauves, grays, greens, violets, and blues, typical of the rocky County Clare countryside.

Note: Patricia Murphy has offered a 10 percent reduction on any items purchased by customers who bring along a copy of *Keep One Suitcase Empty*.

County Mayo

Foxford Woollen Mills Ltd.
Foxford
County Mayo
Tel. (084) 56104

Mon.–Fri. 9:00–5:15 year round; Sat. 10:00–6:00 May–Sept.
American Express, Diners Club, VISA/Barclaycard, MasterCard/Access
Mail order

I'd be happier with Foxford if its factory prices were discounted more heavily, but what can a passionate shopper do about a company whose wholesale prices are only 20 percent lower than its retail prices!

Nevertheless, Foxford does make lovely Irish wool tweeds, shadow stripes, and plaids, which reflect the palette of the Irish countryside. Foxford's fabrics and accessories are excellent values, even if they are not superb bargains.

Foxford's subtle, elegant wool fabrics in a multitude of colors and patterns run 60 inches wide and cost £7.50 to £10 per yard.

The Foxford Picnic Set is an unusual combination of a pure wool Connemara rug with harness-leather straps and harness-leather carrying handle or shoulder strap, so that it can be rolled up neatly and carried easily, plus a matching scarf, in a variety of tartans, plaids, and shadow checks. At Foxford's factory shop, the set costs £35.95; in Dublin, it costs £45 to £55.

Scarves of pure Saxony wool with rolled fringes measuring 11 by 60 inches cost £5.50 here, around £6.50 in Dublin, and 49- by 49-inch wraps with self-fringes all around cost £21.95 here and around £25 in Dublin; the savings on these items are not great. However, occasionally these and other items may be parts of canceled orders or discontinued lines. Then prices are reduced much more, and Foxford offers real bargains.

COUNTY ROSCOMMON

Curlew Designs
Doon Upper Boyle
County Roscommon
Tel. (079) 62579

Mon.–Fri. 9:00–5:00
Traveler's checks in pounds,
* foreign currency, personal*
* checks with ID*
Mail order

The Curlew Designs workshop, about 25 miles from the Yeats country of Sligo, specializes in hand-knitted sweaters made to the designs of Elaine O'Connor, a finalist in the Irish Young Designer of the Year competition. Her sweaters are made of pure new wool hand-spun on the traditional spinning wheel from her own native sheep in natural whites, grays, and browns, or of many shades of mohair yarn.

Curlew's sweaters, priced in U.S. dollars, range from $65 to $95. Among the 1986 season's beauties were a hand-knitted mohair jacket with Victorian collar and quilted sleeves in warm brown autumn shades or in a rainbow palette for $95, and an updated version of the classic Aran sweater, hand-knitted from natural hand-spun pure wool yarn, for $80.

A good selection of the previous season's sweaters was available at $45–$55. Curlew will also design and knit to order.

For the do-it-yourselfer, hand-spun yarn and knitting kits for Aran and designer sweaters range from $20 to $40, and hand-spun yarn is available at $30 per kilogram.

County Wicklow

Arklow Pottery Limited
South Quay
Arklow
County Wicklow
Tel. (402) 32401

Mon.–Sat. 9:30–1:00,
2:00–5:00 Sept.–May;
Mon.–Sun. 9:30–5:30
June–Aug.
American Express,
VISA/Barclaycard,
MasterCard/Access

Arklow Pottery, manufacturers of Noritake and other brands of earthenware, is the largest tableware producer in Ireland, with 80 percent of its 3.5 million pieces a year exported to the United States, Canada, Great Britain, and Europe.

Of course, a tiny percentage of the pieces produced will be seconds, with barely noticeable flaws, and sales manager Paddy Leonard can help you choose an almost perfect table service at prices more than 65 percent below retail.

A 30-piece service for six—dinner plate, salad plate, soup/cereal bowl, cup, and saucer—in Noritake's Eternal Blush, a pretty pattern of calla lilies on a celadon green background, was only £26.70, including the refundable 25 percent VAT—only 66p per piece! Teapots and coffeepots were only £5.10, casseroles with lids £3–£4.50, and family crest mugs just £1.30.

Country Diary, a charming pattern based on the popular *Country Diary of an Edwardian Lady,* is more detailed and expensive, but worth the price. This pattern is sold separately because many people want only the cups and saucers or other individual pieces. Cups are £6.30, saucers £3.30, salad plates £6.70, dinner plates £10.80, and soup/cereal bowls £6.30—£33.60 per place setting.

Avoca Handweavers

Kilmacanogue
Bray
County Wicklow
Tel. (01) 867466 or
     867482

Mon.–Fri. 9:30–5:30,
Sat.–Sun. 10:00–5:30
American Express,
VISA/Barclaycard,
MasterCard/Access,
traveler's checks in pounds
Mail order

Avoca Handweavers has been making beautiful tweeds since 1723. Colors are reminiscent of the soft Irish countryside and the gentle, rolling Wicklow Mountains.

On a recent visit, women's handwoven tweed jackets were £78.50, and matching skirts, £54.60. Mohair jackets were priced at £85, handwoven tweed capes at £98.90, and brushed wool capes at £81.90.

For men, handwoven tweed jackets sold for £82,

and sweaters, for £52. Charming hand-loomed Irish tweed fedoras were £16.50.

For the home, best buys included a 54- by 72-inch brushed mohair throw for £53.90 and a 54- by 72-inch brushed wool throw for only £30.95.

Don't forget to check the bargain baskets, which contain samples and the previous season's garments. A recent trip turned up an unusual black wool Aran sweater marked down from £59.75 to £29.50 and a white Aran vest with leather buttons reduced from £31.50 to only £15.

Items to buy by the bunch are Avoca's solid cologne fragrances in tiny handmade stoneware pots for only £4.95. Choose from among wild rose, honeysuckle, heather, fuchsia, primrose, and violet.

Children's toys and dolls and wonderful. Large boy and girl dolls wearing Aran sweaters are £17.25. A tweed teddy bear is £15.45, as is a rag doll with auburn hair and felt clothing. A life-size leprechaun costs £21, and a sheep covered with fleece, £18.80.

Handy people will enjoy making garments of Avoca's 60-inch-wide handwoven tweed, which sells for £12.90 per meter. Patchwork kits sell for £7.95. Avoca's yarn ranges from £3 to £4.99 per kilogram.

There are also Avoca outlets in Avoca, Co. Wicklow, and Bunratty, Co. Clare, and an Avoca craft center —Connemara Handcrafts—in Letterfrack, County Galway.

Calary Products

Calary House
Ballinastoe
Roundwood
Bray
County Wicklow
Tel. (01) 819198

By appointment
Traveler's checks in pounds,
  U.S. dollars, other
  currencies by prior
  arrangement
No mail order, but will ship
  your purchases

Calary Products, a manufacturer of designer knitwear for ladies and men, is located in the beautiful Wicklow Mountains, on the main road from Bray to the tourist "must" at Glendalough.

Designer and owner Jon Jameson always has stock available, including the previous season's designs and colors, samples, and frequently one-of-a-kind exhibition and fashion-show garments. Jameson gives prices in U.S. dollars and says that his prices for visitors are wholesale or less: between one-third and one-half the Irish retail price. Unisex sweaters start at around $60, jackets are about $85, and women's two-piece suits are priced at about $70, with three- and four-piece suits from $90 to $100. Coordinating hand-knitted pure wool hats are around $8, and scarves, around $13.

Calary produces many different original designs per season in a large range of glowing colors: 12 unisex hand-knitted sweaters and coordinating hand-loomed sweaters, cardigans, jackets, and hats; ladies' skirts, sweaters, cardigans, and vests in a lighter weight of wool in a variety of colors to mix and match.

Heather Wools Ltd.

The Square
Rathdrum
County Wicklow
Tel. (0404) 46410 or
46452 or 46484

Mon.–Fri. 9:00–5:30
Traveler's checks in pounds,
foreign currency
Mail order

Heather Wools manufactures 100 percent Irish Aran wools in 31 delicious colors from $30 per kilogram. There are 15 solid colors: natural cream, natural gray, white, black, emerald, olive, spruce, gold, tan, brown, red, wine, medium blue, dark turquoise, and navy. The 16 tweed colors are more subtle and more difficult to describe because of their intricate blend of colors. Among the prettiest are an emerald/sapphire, a dark red with hints of dark green and brown, and an orange/brown mixture.

Heather Wools also carries a large selection of sample designer Aran sweaters, mostly in sizes 34 to 38 inches, in 100 percent wool, with prices starting at $70.

L'ENVOI

Reader, dear reader, come home with me now,
Our shopping was lovely, the bargains were great;
But it's time now to save up more money somehow
For volume II—Europe—I hope you can't wait.